HISTORIC NEW MEXICO
CHURCHES

HISTORIC NEW MEXICO
CHURCHES

ANNIE LUX

PHOTOGRAPHS BY
DANIEL NADELBACH

Gibbs Smith, Publisher
TO ENRICH AND INSPIRE HUMANKIND
Salt Lake City | Charleston | Santa Fe | Santa Barbara

First Edition
11 10 09 08 07   5 4 3 2 1

Published by
Gibbs Smith, Publisher
P.O. Box 667
Layton, Utah 84041

1.800.835.4993 orders
www.gibbs-smith.com

Designed and produced by Rudy Ramos
Printed and bound in China

Library of Congress Cataloging-in-Publication Data

Lux, Annie.
Historic New Mexico churches / Annie Lux ;
photographs by Daniel Nadelbach. — 1st ed.
    p. cm.
Includes bibliographical references.
ISBN-13: 978-1-4236-0169-2
ISBN-10: 1-4236-0169-6
1. Church architecture—New Mexico.
2. Church decoration and ornament—New Mexico.
I. Title.

NA5230.N6L89 2007
726'.0972—dc22
                                   2007011507

For my mother, who would have liked this book.

And for Lloyd Zusman and Dena Santoro—
I couldn't have done it without you.

Contents

Acknowledgments

This book would not have been possible without the help and support of many people. Marina Ochoa, Curator of the Patrimony for the Arts for the Archdiocese of Santa Fe, gave invaluable help by granting me permission to write about and photograph the churches of northern New Mexico, as well as providing information and encouragement. Many individuals shared with me their time, assistance, and stories. Among them: Christian Andersson and Richard Linsley of Loretto Chapel; Brother Lester Lewis of San Miguel Chapel; Gail Delgado of the Santuario de Guadalupe; Arden Kucate and Tom Campbell of Zuni Pueblo; Juan (Johnny) Casias of Ohkay Owingeh; Bruce Vallo, Janet Reilly, Tribal Interpreter Jody Vallo, and Lyndell Lowden of Acoma Pueblo; Peter Pino, Tammy Pino, and Governor Rudy Shije of Zia Pueblo; Father Francis Malley of San Francisco de Asís in Ranchos de Taos; Father John McHugh of St. Gertrude's in Mora; Norma Pinada of the Salinas National Monument; Willie Atencío of Santa Cruz; Susie Romero Gurule of Truchas; José L. Lopez of Las Trampas; Richard Archuleta of Taos Pueblo; Annie Anaya of Socorro; Patty Guggino of Los Lentes. Thanks also to Eric Faust, and Elizabeth West and the Santa Fe Public Library for help with architectural terms.

I'm grateful to everyone at Gibbs Smith, Publisher—particularly Suzanne Taylor (editorial director), Madge Baird (managing editor), Linda Nimori (project editor), Leslie Stitt (associate editor), Jared Smith (assistant editor), Renee Wald (assistant production editor), Courtney Rottgering (publicist), Rudy Ramos (book designer)—and to Ellen Kleiner of Blessingway Authors' Services for getting the ball rolling.

My thanks also to Daniel Nadelbach, whose excellent photography illustrates the historical data so well.

And I'm especially thankful for all my friends who helped me through the process of creating this book, especially Margot Avery and her family, and Todd Welsh, who provided sanctuary of a less church-like sort; Angela Tipton, my "church-spotting" companion; and Michael French, Dena Santoro, Louis Mello, Gwendolyn Wells, and Hillary Welles, who gave the kind of assistance and support that only friends who are also writers can give.

Introduction

In New Mexico, historic churches are as much a part of the cultural landscape as adobe and green chile. In Santa Fe alone you'll find Archbishop Lamy's
grand Cathedral of St. Francis and the San Miguel Chapel (known as the Oldest
Church in the United States), as well as the Loretto Chapel with its miraculous staircase and the Santuario de Guadalupe with its famous altar screen. At some of the
pueblos, four-hundred-year-old churches stand amid structures sometimes hundreds
of years older. And if you drive the back
roads and byways of the state, as I did
while researching this book, you'll see
others—the smaller churches, the roadside chapels, the occasional larger
church for what is (or once was) a larger
community. They're everywhere.

What I came to realize while
putting this book together is that to
tell the story of these historic churches

is to tell the story of New Mexico. Some of the state's oldest buildings are churches, built by the native Indians under the supervision of Franciscan missionaries. For Spain, the conquest of new lands and the spreading of Christianity were inextricable, perhaps because Pope Alexander VI charged Spain with the task of converting the New World almost immediately after Columbus returned from his 1492 voyage. The Spanish Crown took this charge seriously. Priests and friars of the Order of St. Francis began arriving in "New Spain" less than ten years after Cortés conquered Mexico. For these dedicated Catholic missionaries, "Christianizing" meant more than preaching the gospel to the natives. It meant building churches.

One of these Franciscans, a friar named Marcos de Niza, was among the very first Europeans to see New Mexico. In 1539, he returned from a journey through the western mesas where the Zuni Indians made their home and regaled the governor of New Spain with tales of marvelous cities made of gold in the land he called the "New Kingdom of St. Francis." The next year, Francisco Vásquez de Coronado launched a massive expedition to explore the territory now known as New Mexico.

We'll never know what Fray Marcos actually saw: was it the desert sun bathing the Indians' adobe houses in light so intense that they shone like gold? Was he duped by stories told him by the Zuni, who hoped to send him off on a wild-goose chase? Or did he make it all up, wanting the chance to Christianize the natives of New Mexico and needing the backing of the Spanish Crown to do so? Despite a two-year search, Coronado's conquistadors found no gold. What they found instead was New Mexico—a land of haunting desert vistas that gentled into greener mountainous landscapes farther north, a land peopled by natives living in villages the Spanish called *pueblos*.

When Spain finally opened New Mexico to settlement in 1598, twelve Franciscans journeyed north with the first settlement party. They divided the territory between them and immediately set out for the pueblos and founded missions. What men these early Franciscans must have been! While the conquistadors searched for riches and fame, the missionaries were after a different gold: souls. Whatever one might think of their task, their faith and dedication cannot be questioned. They set

off alone into a strange land, among strange people whose language they didn't speak, knowing full well that the tasks ahead of them were near impossible at best and that, at worst, a martyr's death might await them. Yet it was not only their courage that set these men apart—it was also their knowledge. Setting up a mission involved more than teaching Christianity—more, even, than building churches, which they were expected to know how to do. These Franciscans and those who followed them also taught the Indians to speak and sing in Spanish, to weave and to work with metals. They introduced wheat and barley and new methods of farming. They sometimes even taught the Indians to play European musical instruments.

Fray Marcos wouldn't be the last Franciscan to give an exaggerated report to the Spanish authorities. The missionaries routinely inflated the numbers of their converts and occasionally wrote of potential riches to be found—all in the hopes of getting the Spanish Crown to fund more missions. It seems they needn't have worried:

by 1630, it was clear to Spain that no real profit was to be found in the New Mexican colony, yet the Spanish king elected to continue the endeavor as a missionary effort.

It does seem strange that it was so easy for the Spanish to move into this territory, for the Franciscans to convert so many so quickly. Yet how marvelous the Spaniards must have appeared to the Indians. With their horses and sheep, rich clothing and supplies—not to mention their firearms—they must have seemed wealthier and more formidable than anything the Indians had ever seen. To them, the white men's gods must have seemed powerful indeed. Most tribes in New Mexico had a flexible spiritual belief system and regularly annexed the gods of neighboring tribes. Worshipping the Christian gods alongside their own—which the Franciscans at first encouraged—must have seemed natural in those early days.

Unfortunately, the early civilian settlers—soldiers and officials—were not of the same caliber as those first Franciscans. Many, including the governors, were greedy and cruel, interested only in enslaving the Indians and reaping the fruits of their labor. The Franciscans and the civil authorities came into conflict early and often. It must also be said that the missionaries who came into the territory later in the seventeenth century did not always have motives as pure as those of their predecessors. As time went on, tolerance for the native people's traditional spirituality gradually ceased and the greed of the civil authorities rapidly increased—with the Indians usually caught between the factions. Resentment against both groups finally exploded in the 1680 Pueblo Revolt, when the territory's natives drove the Spanish out of New Mexico for the next twelve years. Most of the churches built before that date were either completely destroyed or badly damaged.

The settlers who came to New Mexico with Don Diego de Vargas after his 1692 reconquest were a different breed. These were not glory-seekers but families wanting land and homes, people prepared for the arduous adventure awaiting them. De Vargas, too, was made of better stuff than the governors who came before him. A sincerely devout and fair man, he promised the Indians that there would be no more forced labor, that the new Franciscans who (naturally) accompanied him would be more tolerant of their beliefs, and that their rights to their lands would be

respected. While these promises weren't kept entirely (especially as time went on), with a few notable exceptions they were mostly honored.

It was at this time that the next era of church building in New Mexico began. Most of the mission churches were rebuilt and, as the territory grew, churches went up in the small Spanish communities that were founded to accommodate the new settlers. These churches were not part of the missionary effort and so were not supported by the Spanish Crown. The people of these new settlements had to finance and build—and decorate—their churches themselves. This was the age of the *santeros*, the local craftspeople and artists who created the folk art for which New Mexico churches of this era are celebrated.

Yet another chapter dawned in the spiritual life of New Mexico after the 1848 Treaty of Guadalupe Hidalgo gave the territory of New Mexico to the United States. With the arrival of New Mexico's first bishop, Jean Baptiste Lamy, another era of church building began, this one informed by a European sensibility. The Romanesque-style Cathedral of St. Francis in Santa Fe is the most obvious example of this trend, which also explains the brick Gothic structure at Ohkay Owingeh (formerly San Juan Pueblo) on the site where the first church in New Mexico likely stood. Forty-five new churches were built during Archbishop Lamy's tenure, and many older structures were renovated to include European-style elements.

In recent decades, the Spanish Colonial and Pueblo Revival styles have enjoyed a revival in New Mexico. Efforts to preserve and restore the older churches abound, thanks in large part to the famed architect of the Southwest, John Gaw Meem, as well as to organizations dedicated to preservation efforts such as Cornerstones and the Archdiocese of Santa Fe, and to the dedicated grassroots efforts of the communities themselves. Newer churches such as Cristo Rey in Santa Fe and Santo Tomás in Abiquiú honor the best of the old traditions and look as much at home in their surroundings as if they'd been there for centuries.

It would be the work of a lifetime to catalogue all the churches in New Mexico, let alone to record all their stories. It is my hope that the churches included in this volume will begin to tell the story—the story of dreams, of faith, of conflict and reconciliation; the story of New Mexico.

PART ONE

The Cross and the Crown

CHAPTER ONE

God, Gold, and Glory

 Nuestra Señora de Guadalupe Mission, Zuni Pueblo

The Cities of Gold

Like many conquistadors before him, when Francisco Vásquez de Coronado launched the first Spanish exploration party into New Mexico in 1540, he was searching for gold. Instead of the Seven Golden Cities of Cíbola, he found six villages of multistoried adobe houses—and the Zuni, who had been living and farming here for thousands of years. Zuni Pueblo—still the largest and perhaps most traditional in New Mexico—is located in the western part of the state near the town of Gallup, in a landscape of mesas and crags so dramatic and mystical, it's no wonder that the early Spanish explorers believed the tales of "riches beyond compare" to be found there. Unfortunately, the legendary Cities of Gold were just that: legends. It must have been quite a disappointment for Coronado. Thirsty after the long dry trek, low on food, their expectations dashed—what must the Spaniards have thought of these humble people in their villages made of mud?

What the Zuni thought of these strange invaders—three hundred Spanish soldiers, more than a thousand Mexican Indians, plus a handful of slaves and four

Facing: Mesa lands at Acoma, west-central New Mexico.

3

Franciscan missionaries—can only be imagined. Certainly they were unimpressed by Coronado's demand (the usual *requirimiento* given by conquistadors to soon-to-be-conquered natives) that the Zuni submit to the authority of the Spanish Crown and "acknowledge the authority of the [Catholic] Church as the ruler of the whole world. . . ." In any case, the first meeting between the natives of New Mexico and the conquistadors was a violent one: when the Spanish party—in dire need of food—was denied entrance to the Zuni village of Hawikuh, Coronado took it by force. The Zuni were compelled to host the conquistador and feed and shelter his men until it became clear that no gold was to be found in the Zuni villages. Coronado's party moved on in their search, exploring much of New Mexico as well as parts of Arizona and the plains as far east as Kansas over the next two years.

Thanks to the Coronado expedition's failure to find gold anywhere in the territory, the native people of New Mexico were left in relative peace for the next fifty years. In fact, its remote location also spared the Zuni villages from contact with the first wave of Catholic missionaries who accompanied Don Juan Oñate's settlement party in 1598. Eventually, though, in 1629, a new group of Franciscans arrived from Spain, ready to expand the Christianizing crusade in the "New Kingdom of St. Francis." Before long, several of these missionaries appeared at Zuni, where they built churches in two of the villages. The mission church at Hawikuh was called La Purísima Concepción (Immaculate Conception); an identical sister-church was built at the village of Hálona—the "Middle Place," which is now the heart of the Zuni Pueblo—and was originally dedicated as Nuestra Señora de la Candelaria (Our Lady of Candelaria).

The multistoried adobe houses of the old Zuni villages no longer exist. These adobe high-rises are at Taos Pueblo.

Relations between the Spanish and the Zuni continued to be difficult. The Zuni had their own very complicated sets of beliefs, ceremonies, and rituals, and resented the interference of the Spanish missionaries. Zuni was known to be the most difficult of the pueblos in terms of the conversion efforts. Priests who requested the assignment were among the most zealous. Some expressed a desire for the glory of martyrdom—a wish that several would be granted. In 1632, the newly arrived Fray Francisco Letrado, known for his fervor, reprimanded his Zuni "converts" for not attending Mass. The Zuni turned on him, pelting him with arrows as he fell to his knees. Another missionary to the Zuni, Fray Martin de Arvada, met a similar fate.

Drought and attacks by nomadic Apache and Navajo tribes—scourges that would plague the territory for years to come—only added to the strain. A particularly fierce raid in 1672 led to the abandonment of the mission at Hawikuh. Marauders dragged Fray Pedro de Avila y Ayala from the church, smashed his skull with the church's bell, and then burned the church. (Though blamed on the Apaches, there are some reports that the Zuni may have also participated in this attack.) Eight years later, when the Zuni joined their neighboring tribes in the Pueblo Revolt, yet another priest met his martyrdom: Fray Juan del Val was killed while standing before the altar at La Purísima Concepción.

Nuestra Señora de Guadalupe Mission Church

Unlike most of the early pueblo missions, the church at Zuni wasn't destroyed in the Pueblo Revolt, though it was badly damaged. In the years after the revolt, the Zuni abandoned Hálona and sought refuge in a mountain fortress. But that may not be the only reason for the building's survival. Despite the decades of strain and hostility, Zuni was the only pueblo that didn't destroy everything belonging to the Spanish missionaries. In fact, when peace was reestablished after 1692, sacred vessels and other church property were found to have been carefully preserved. The Zuni returned to Hálona, where the mission church was rebuilt and renamed in honor of Our Lady of Guadalupe. The church has an exterior balcony and a curved bell tower in the center of the façade, though the towers at either side suggest that two more belfries may have originally been intended.

The Spanish Crown's support for the missions ceased when Mexico won its independence in 1821. Despite the efforts of the Zuni people, the church fell into disrepair. Considered one of the finest examples of early Spanish Colonial architecture in New Mexico, Nuestra Señora de Guadalupe Mission Church has nonetheless suffered periods of neglect as well as several attempts at repair and remodeling. At one point, in an attempt at preservation, the adobe church was covered in stucco, with less than happy results. The church, also known as the Old Zuni Mission, has been deconsecrated and is now administered by the Zuni tribe, who hope to restore the lovely historic building.

The Kachina Murals

Today, the Old Zuni Mission is best known for a more recent addition: a mural project on the interior walls begun by Zuni artist Alex Seowtewa and continued to this day by family artists. The mural depicts Zuni kachina figures—religious figures

The Old Zuni Mission: Nuestra Señora de Guadalupe.

in traditional costume—and completely covers the walls on both sides of the nave. The murals have been a source of controversy from both sides of the fence. Despite an atmosphere of tolerance between traditional native spirituality and the Catholic Church in New Mexico today, there are some who say the mural is inappropriate. "What are Zuni religious figures doing on the walls of a Catholic church?" ask some conservative Catholic officials. Some Zuni elders ask the same question. Many, however, celebrate the blending of the two cultures. In any case, there is no denying that the murals—colorful, life-size, beautiful—represent quite an achievement, but, like the church itself, it is an achievement in need of preservation and repair, as the interior walls of the church are becoming water-damaged.

The Stolen Statue

In 1775, a Spanish cartographer named Bernardo Miero y Pacheco carved *bultos* (wooden statues) of two archangels for Nuestra Señora de Guadalupe. For many years, San Gabriel and San Miguel guarded either side of the altar screen until the statues were stolen under dark of night by James Stevenson, a Union soldier, in 1880. The bultos reappeared at the Smithsonian Institution in Washington, D.C., where the San Gabriel statue was destroyed in a fire. Thanks to efforts initiated by former Zuni governor Robert E. Lewis, the San Miguel bulto was returned to its New Mexico home in 2004. It is currently on display at the Visitor Center at Zuni Pueblo.

Bulto (*wooden statue*) of San Miguel, home again at Zuni Pueblo.

San Juan de los Caballeros, Ohkay Owingeh

The "Gentle People"

The first capital of New Mexico wasn't at Santa Fe but at a small settlement near the Indian village of Ohkay Owingeh. Almost sixty years passed after the Coronado expedition before the territory of New Mexico was declared officially open for settlement. In 1598, Don Juan de Oñate—appointed first governor of New Mexico by King Phillip II of Spain—set out from Mexico and headed north. This wasn't an exploration expedition but a settlement party: many of the four hundred men with Oñate brought their families. They also brought sheep, goats, cattle, supplies in eighty-three wagons—and ten Franciscans, who came to New Mexico to found missions among the Indian pueblos. It was a long, slow trip across the barren deserts of the southern part of the territory, through what would later be called the Jornada del Muerto—Journey of the Dead Man—before the settlers reached the gentler landscapes of the high deserts. Ohkay Owingeh must have seemed a paradise after their dry journey: it is a beautiful spot near the confluence of the Rio Grande and Rio

The land where San Gabriel once stood is now an empty field on the pueblo of Ohkay Owingeh. All signs of the Spanish settlement were destroyed in the 1680 Pueblo Revolt.

Chama, not far from the Jemez Mountains. The people of the village welcomed the Spanish party, providing them with food and shelter for the winter. At Oñate's request, the tribe also gave them a piece of land of their own. Yunque-Yunque, just across the Rio Grande from the heart of Ohkay Owingeh, became San Gabriel, the first capital of New Mexico. Oñate acknowledged their kindness and his own patron saint by renaming the village San Juan de los Caballeros—Saint John of the Gentle People. The village was known as San Juan Pueblo until 2005, when the tribe voted to reclaim its original name of Ohkay Owingeh, which means Place of the Strong People.

San Juan de los Caballeros

The first church in New Mexico, San Juan de los Caballeros (also known as San Juan Bautista or St. John the Baptist), was built at San Juan Pueblo in September 1598; it was completely destroyed in the Pueblo Revolt of 1680. Some years after the 1692 reconquest, a second adobe church, which stood on the village plaza for almost three hundred years, was built there. Today on that site stands a Gothic-inspired brick church that might seem more at home in a French village than among the adobe houses and unpaved streets of a New Mexico pueblo.

The 1850 arrival of Jean Baptiste Lamy, the first bishop of the newly created Vicariate of Santa Fe, ushered in a new era of church architecture in New Mexico. Bishop Lamy, a Frenchman, preferred European styles to the traditional Spanish Colonial–style churches. Most of the French priests he brought to New Mexico shared his prejudice. In 1899, a small stone chapel dedicated to Our Lady of Lourdes was built across the plaza from San Juan Bautista by one of this new breed, Father Camille Seux. A priest much beloved by the people of San Juan Pueblo, "Father Camillo" also used his own funds to build the church that stands on the pueblo today. The old adobe church was razed to make way for the new structure, which must have reminded Father Seux of his home. The brick church has a gothic arched door-way, pitched roof, and stained glass windows. Although there are now many Gothic and Romanesque churches in New Mexico (the most famous being the Cathedral of

Facing:
San Juan de los
Caballeros Church,
Ohkay Owingeh.

St. Francis in Santa Fe), San Juan Pueblo—Ohkay Owingeh—is the only pueblo with a church of this style.

Popé and the Pueblo Revolt

The early fellowship between Oñate's settlers and the gentle people of San Juan didn't take long to wear thin. The gifts of food and goods given to the Spanish when they first arrived became expected tributes that the Spaniards regularly demanded from the Indians. Oñate himself—who by all accounts was anything but gentle—very quickly fell from favor with both the Indians and the Spanish Crown. It soon became obvious that New Mexico's first governor was more interested in searching for wealth for himself than in governing a new territory or overseeing Spain's missionary efforts. For these reasons as well as for more specific abuses of his authority (including a disastrous and cruel incident at Acoma Pueblo), Oñate was removed from his office in 1609. The new governor, Don Pedro de Peralta, moved the capital from San Gabriel to Santa Fe, though many settlers and the missionaries assigned to the San Juan Mission remained behind.

At San Juan and elsewhere, the greed of the conquistadors caused resentment among the native people, who were often forced into labor to support the soldiers and the missionaries. Worst of all, the Spanish were eroding the natives' way of life. The Franciscans had zealously taken to their task of converting the Indians to Christianity and establishing missions at most of the pueblos. Initially the natives seemed to take to the new religion, in most cases incorporating it into their own beliefs. The missionaries encouraged this at first. As time went on, however, the Franciscans pressured the natives to abandon their old beliefs and rituals and to worship an exclusively Christian god. Dances and other traditional native ceremonies were forbidden and the Indians' sacred objects were destroyed. In 1675, forty-seven Pueblo medicine men were arrested and accused of practicing witchcraft. Four were sentenced to death; the rest were publicly whipped. Among these prisoners was a man named Popé.

Though some accounts credit Taos Pueblo with producing the man who organized the natives of New Mexico in the most successful Indian uprising in

American history, Popé (sometimes spelled Popay) was born at San Juan Pueblo. Over the years, rebellions against the Spaniards were often discussed on the few occasions—trade markets, feast days—when the different tribes came together. A few small uprisings were attempted but were easily quashed. Before 1680, there wasn't much unity between the tribes of New Mexico. Each pueblo considered itself a separate nation, and relations were often riddled with rivalries and suspicion. It took a leader of great conviction and charisma to bring the pueblos together. That leader was Popé.

From Taos Pueblo—the northernmost of the pueblos, far from the eyes of Spanish authorities—he planned the Pueblo Revolt. On August 10, 1680, the Pueblo Indians of New Mexico rose up against the Spanish. Hundreds of settlers and soldiers, as well as twenty-one Franciscans, were killed. The rest fled south to El Paso del Norte (present-day El Paso, Texas). At San Juan and elsewhere, churches were burned and most evidence of the Spanish presence was destroyed. At San Juan Pueblo, the only remaining Spanish object was the cane given to the pueblo by the King of Spain, which is still passed down to each succeeding pueblo governor.

Popé's mission was to turn back the clock and return the pueblos to the way of life they had been leading before the Spanish came. He declared himself the new governor of New Mexico and forbade the use of anything Spanish: their language, their religion, the crops they had introduced. He even ordered the Spanish settlers' fruit trees cut down and their sheep slaughtered. Not everyone agreed; some pueblos continued to plant the "forbidden seeds" of wheat and barley. Before long, resentment against Popé's despotic demands erupted, and rifts between the pueblos—never closely aligned to begin with—grew greater.

After Popé's death twelve years later, a new conquistador, Don Diego de Vargas, reconquered New Mexico. Inevitably, more missionaries came with him. By then many of the pueblos weren't opposed to their return. During the decades of Spanish rule, they had come to rely on Spanish protection from the raids of the nomadic Plains Indians. And in many respects, of course, life had improved for the Indians under the Spanish. Undoubtedly, there must have been the additional realization that they couldn't launch another successful revolt. Then there was De Vargas himself. By most accounts a great and gallant leader, he assured the natives of New Mexico that there would be no more tribute or forced labor demanded of them, and that their traditional beliefs would be respected by the new breed of Franciscans under his command.

 **San Esteban del Rey, Acoma Pueblo**

The City in the Sky

According to their legend, the Acoma people originally lived on Enchanted Mesa, a beautiful four-hundred-foot-high rock in what is now central New Mexico. Every morning the people came down off the mesa to farm in the valley. Every evening they climbed the steep stairway path back to their village. One day, a great storm— sudden and terrible—tore through the land. Wind and rain eroded the footholds of the path, destroying the only access to their homes. On that day, three women had remained behind on the mesa. When the storm cleared, they crept out of their houses and looked down at their friends and families in the valley below. The women realized with horror that they were stranded on top of Enchanted Mesa; the only way down was to jump. Some say they hoped to survive the fall and rejoin their people. Others think they jumped rather than slowly starving alone in the empty village. The Acoma people never returned to Enchanted Mesa, choosing instead to rebuild their homes on the nearby mesa where the village now stands.

Acoma Pueblo claims to be the oldest continually inhabited village in the United States. Archaeologists confirm that it is at least eight hundred years old; there is evidence that it may be much older. Built atop a 357-foot rock mesa, it is certainly one of the most unusual. The first Europeans to see Acoma—a splinter group from Coronado's 1540 exploration party—were impressed by the fortress-like village. "The ascent was so difficult that we repented climbing to the top," wrote one soldier. Another later reported that the Acomans "came down to meet us peacefully,

Enchanted Mesa.

although they might have spared themselves the trouble and remained on their rock, for we would have been unable to disturb them in the least."

Unfortunately, peaceful greetings between the Europeans and the Indians at Acoma wouldn't last. Soon after Don Juan Oñate established the settlement at San Gabriel near San Juan Pueblo, exploration parties went out to the nearby villages. One such party arrived at Acoma in December 1598. Some stories say that the party, under the command of Oñate's nephew Juan de Zaldivar, was refused entrance to the village. Another version holds that the Acomans invited the Spanish onto the mesa, promising food and supplies, and that the Indians then ambushed them. What is clear is that the Acoma people refused to promise obedience to the Spanish Crown, and that the Acoma warriors attacked the party, killing Zaldivar and all but a few of his men.

News of the slaughter reached Don Juan at San Gabriel all too soon. The angry governor declared war on Acoma. The retaliation party, led by Zaldivar's younger brother Vicente, was heavily armed. The battle that ensued lasted three days and left hundreds of Acoma warriors dead. They had no choice but to surrender, but that didn't satisfy Oñate. He ordered that the left foot of every male over the age of twenty-five be cut off, and sentenced all the surviving Acoma people to twenty years of slavery.

The sentences of slavery were commuted at the urging of the Franciscan priests. Possibly they felt some responsibility for the terrible carnage, having advised the governor to wage war on Acoma. Before sending the avenging party, Oñate had consulted Fray Alonzo Martinez, who gave him his blessing. Said the priest, "If the cause of war is . . . peace in the kingdom, [one] may justly wage war and destroy any

obstacle in the way of peace until it is effectively achieved." Oñate certainly felt that there would be no peace in the land as long as there was rebellion against the Spanish Crown; he probably believed that a strong show of brute force would discourage rebellion from the other Indian villages. But nothing could justify the savagery of Oñate's revenge. The Battle of Acoma marked the beginning of the conflict and resentment that would explode many years later in the Pueblo Revolt. It is cold comfort to know that Oñate's brutality ultimately cost him his appointment as governor of New Mexico. He was ordered to return to Mexico City, where he stood trial for his actions at Acoma and for other offenses, and was banished from New Mexico.

Today, only a handful of people live full-time in the mesa-top village, which lacks electricity and running water. Most Acomans have homes in nearby towns, spending time on the mesa in the summer and on feast days. Access to the top of the

Acoma Pueblo.

mesa became easier after a road was built by a Hollywood studio in 1929; several westerns have been filmed at Acoma. A new Visitors and Cultural Center was opened in 2006.

San Esteban del Rey

It is said that the Spanish built the mission church at Acoma as a gesture of peace. Perhaps that's true, but it's also true that churches were being built at many of the pueblos during the same period. And it is certainly true that San Esteban del Rey—like all the pueblo mission churches—was built by the forced labor of the native people.

Begun in 1629 and completed in 1640, San Esteban del Rey (St. Stephen the King) is the only existing pueblo mission church to make it through the 1680 Pueblo Revolt unscathed, perhaps because Acoma's location kept the church far from the worst of the fighting, which primarily took place farther north. Undoubtedly the massive structure was useful as a fortress: a good thing to have if your primary fortress (the location at the top of the high flat rock) is infiltrated by invaders. Possibly, it's been suggested, its very size would have made it difficult to destroy. In addition, there must have been the memory—none too distant—of the eleven years of monumental labor it took to build it.

All the building materials had to be brought up from the valley to the top of the mesa. Thousands of tons of earth, stone, and water were carried in baskets up the steep narrow footpaths that provided the only access to the village. Fourteen enormous timbers for the roof beams were harvested from the forests of Mount Taylor, some forty miles away in the San Mateo Mountains, and hauled on the shoulders of Acoma men, who never allowed the timbers to touch the ground. It is said that when the roof beams (*vigas*) were being put into place, one of them did fall and touch the church's earthen floor. Rather than allow it a lofty place in the church's ceiling, the offending beam was pressed into service elsewhere in the building.

The result of this massive undertaking was a 21,000-square-foot mission church with walls nine feet thick in places. The church has a single-nave plan with towers on either side of its east-facing façade. The mission complex also included a

commodious *convento* (priest's residence) and a cemetery in front of the church. It is guarded by sculpted mud heads that line the top of the retaining wall around the church and cemetery. Some say the heads represent the warriors who fell at the Battle of Acoma. Others, who hold that the people of Acoma prefer not to dwell on the darker aspects of their past, say they are benevolent spirits who watch over the pueblo.

San Esteban del Rey, Acoma Pueblo. Note the sculpted heads along the top of the wall.

The Good Priest

Several priests had been assigned to Acoma Pueblo in the days following the Battle of Acoma, but all refused out of fear. Finally, in 1629, Fray Juan Ramirez bravely made his way to the Sky City. As he attempted to climb the mesa, the villagers jeered at him and pelted him with stones and arrows. In the excitement, a woman in the crowd dropped her child over the side of the mesa. In some versions of the story, Fray Juan caught the child—an infant—in his robes. In others, the priest prayed over the injured child, a little girl, and the child revived. In all versions, the event was declared a miracle and Fray Juan Ramirez was welcomed into the village of Acoma, where he remained as their pastor for more than thirty years. It was he who oversaw the building of San Esteban del Rey.

The Bad Priest

Not quite so beloved was one of Fray Juan's successors, Fray Baltazar Montoya, who was immortalized in Willa Cather's classic novel *Death Comes for the Archbishop*. In Cather's story, the greedy and sensual priest demands that the Acoma people live to serve him, to tend his elaborate gardens, and to provide him with the best of meats and material goods, all at the expense of the well-being of their own families. When in a fit of pique he kills a young boy who has been pressed into domestic service, the people have had enough. They take the priest from the convento and, swinging him by his hands and feet, hurl him over the side of the mesa. In other versions of the story, the priest isn't tossed over the side but chased there by the angry people. The spot where he fell is—like Enchanted Mesa—considered cursed and is avoided by the Acoma people.

 # Nuestra Señora de la Asunción, Zia Pueblo

Zia Pueblo

The ancestors of the Zia people began migrating south from Chaco Canyon and Mesa Verde around AD 1250, looking for more fertile lands for their agrarian society. They settled here, about thirty-five miles northwest of Albuquerque, on a small mesa nestled in the valley of the Sierra Nacimiento Mountains. Zia's mesa isn't as tall

Landscape, Zia Pueblo.

or dramatic as Acoma's, but its village of small houses made of cobblestone and mud has its own charm. When the Spanish first saw Zia, it had a thriving population between seven and fifteen thousand. Today it numbers well under one thousand, but the pueblo—one of the few that has made no concessions to tourism—is well kept and unspoiled.

Coronado himself was among the first Europeans to visit the village; in early 1541, he made his winter quarters nearby along the banks of the Rio Grande. The people of Zia were welcoming and generous to the party, and friendly relations were established. Coronado even left four bronze cannons in the care of the village when he set off that spring on his fruitless search for the elusive Cities of Gold.

Nuestra Señora de la Asunción Mission

Zia was among the earliest missions established by the Franciscans accompanying Don Juan de Oñate. Recent archeological studies have shown that the church at Zia is much older than previously thought. Although it was badly damaged in the Pueblo Revolt, it must not have been completely destroyed, as a recent study has dated parts of the existing structure back to 1610. The church was rebuilt after 1692 and has undergone several renovations.

Unlike most pueblos (and other Spanish towns in New Mexico), Zia's church, Nuestra Señora de la Asunción (Our Lady of the Assumption), isn't built on the main plaza. Rather, it perches at the northern end of the village near the edge of the mesa. To build the church, adobe bricks were made down in the valley and sent up to the mesa by a human chain three-quarters of a mile long. The people of the village regularly plastered the building with mud until 1972, when the adobe church was covered with stucco in an effort to preserve it better. This is a process that has fallen into disfavor, primarily because stucco can trap moisture underneath and inside the church (as happened at the Old Zuni Mission). The stucco was removed twenty years later, but it was found that the process had been much more successful here than in other churches. In 1998, the church was re-stuccoed. Today the Spanish Colonial–style church is beautifully whitewashed. The façade is decorated with

paintings of horses on either side of the front door. The murals are the work of Ralph Aragon, a local artist, and depict the yellow and white horses special to Zia Pueblo.

The Battle of Zia

Although relations between the Spanish and the people of Zia seemed better than those at other pueblos, the Zia joined their neighboring tribes in the Pueblo Revolt—with devastating results for the tribe. Another disastrous encounter with the Spanish came five years before the successful 1692 reconquest of New Mexico, when another Spanish general, Reneros de Posada, attempted to reenter the territory. A battle was fought between the Spanish and the Indians from Zia and surrounding pueblos. The Spanish won easily and losses at Zia were great. In addition to the battle casualties, many others were taken prisoner and still others were executed. Perhaps this is the reason why, in 1692, the people of Zia and nearby Santa Ana Pueblo not only made no resistance but actually welcomed Don Diego de Vargas's army with great ceremony. In fact, the Zia became great allies of the Spanish and helped them quell any dissent to what has been called (not entirely accurately) the peaceful reconquest of New Mexico.

The Mass Baptism

More Franciscans journeyed to New Mexico with De Vargas and picked up their Christianizing efforts where they had left off twelve years earlier. At many of the pueblos, mass baptisms were performed. At Zia, this mass baptism was performed on the very day that De Vargas took possession of the pueblo in the name of the King of Spain. The priests who accompanied him not only baptized the not-yet-converted, they also pronounced a general absolution to all the Zia people, welcoming them back into the faith. The white cross that stands in the plaza at Zia commemorates this event.

The Bell in the Mesa

In the 1700s, the Zia mission church possessed a bell that was the envy of all the missions. Its loud, clear peals could be heard as far as Santa Ana, some seventeen miles away. There came—as there all too often does in New Mexico—a long period of

Facing:
Nuestra Señora de la Asunción, Zia Pueblo.

The white cross in the Zia Pueblo plaza commemorates the mass baptism performed by Franciscan missionaries with Don Diego de Vargas in 1692.

drought. Crops failed; food was scarce. To supplement their prayers for rain, the people of Zia decided to sacrifice their greatest treasure: their magnificent bell. It was taken down from its tower at Nuestra Señora de la Asunción Church and buried deep in the side of the mesa. As far as anyone knows, it's still there.

San Agustín Mission, Isleta Pueblo

Isleta Pueblo

In 1540, Coronado himself visited the village its inhabitants called Shiewhibak (which refers to a small knife used in an old ceremonial game). He didn't find gold here either; he did, however, name the thriving pueblo on the banks of the Rio Grande Isleta (Little Island) after a small point of land that projected into the river.

The people of Isleta have been living on this site—about thirteen miles south of present-day Albuquerque—since the early 1300s. By the early 1600s, Isleta was one of the largest missions in the territory, with an impressive church, its own parish priest, and a population of more than two thousand, thanks in part to refugees—both Indian and Spanish—seeking shelter from Apache raids. Probably because of the high population of Spaniards in the latter part of the 1600s, the

Spanish here weren't harmed or killed during the Pueblo Revolt as they were at most pueblos. In fact, the Spanish governor was so confident of their loyalty that he designated Isleta Pueblo as the meeting place for all the evacuating Spanish. After fleeing Santa Fe, though, he found the pueblo deserted. The Spanish at Isleta, fearing the governor dead, had already headed south, taking many of the Indians with them. Others Isletans fled west to Arizona and lived among the Hopi.

Most say the Isleta people never joined the Pueblo Revolt, that they were prevented from doing so by the large number of Spanish soldiers occupying their village. One story, though, tells that in 1681, during the first failed reconquest attempt by the Spanish, the Isleta Indians pledged loyalty to the Spanish governor but were secretly allied with the other native tribes. When the governor, Antonio de Otermín, learned of their deceit, he burned the church and the pueblo and took all the natives of Isleta prisoner. The latter part of the story doesn't seem to be true: Otermín wrote in a 1681 report that when he returned to Isleta Pueblo, he found the church already "burned and ruined." The people there, he said, welcomed the Spanish back and surrendered their "idols, feathers, powders, masks, and every other thing pertaining to their idolatry and superstition." They likely had little choice: Otermín arrived at Isleta with one hundred and forty heavily armed soldiers. When the soldiers left to return to El Paso del Norte, they took the Indians of Isleta with them. There they founded a second village, Isleta-del-Sur, which still exists as Ysleta, Texas.

San Agustín de la Isleta Mission

Isleta Pueblo's original mission church—dedicated to San Antonio—was built on the east side of Isleta's plaza during the first spate of mission building in the first years of the seventeenth century. The church was built of adobe bricks made of earth dug right at the building site. San Antonio was all but destroyed in the years after the revolt. A new church was built on the same spot, this time named San Agustín de la Isleta. Known as St. Augustine, it is still an impressive and beautiful church. Although it has undergone many renovations over the years, the whitewashed church retains many traditional features, including a clerestory window, exterior buttresses, and twin towers.

Padre Padilla's Coffin

In one version of this strange story, the casket buried in St. Augustine Church belongs to New Mexico's first Catholic martyr. When Coronado abandoned his search for gold and returned to Mexico in 1542, two of the Franciscans in his company—Juan de Padilla and Luís de Escalena—chose to remain behind to convert the natives. With so much ground to cover, the two priests separated; Padre Padilla headed east toward Isleta and Quivera, where he was killed by natives. According to this version of the story, somehow the priest's body was taken from Quivera to Isleta where, after the church was built many years later, it was laid to rest in a grave near the altar. Once a year, it was said, the coffin rose up out of the ground beneath the altar so that all could view the mummified body. It is even said that some took "souvenirs" from these events: pieces of the padre's clothing, which were said to have great healing powers.

A more plausible—and better documented—version of the story is recounted in Joe L. Montoya's booklet *Isleta Pueblo and the Church of St. Augustine*. In this version,

San Agustín Mission, Isleta Pueblo.

the "Padre Padilla" buried under the altar isn't the martyr Juan Francisco de Padilla but Father Juan José de Padilla, pastor of the church at Laguna Pueblo, who died while visiting Isleta in 1756. According to a report later found in his casket, the priest was stabbed to death. No other details, however, have come to light, and the reason—if not the method—for Padre Padilla's death remains a mystery. It does seem true that the cottonwood coffin containing the priest's body rose up to the surface of the church's earthen floor several times. The second time, in 1819, the casket was opened and the body inside was found to be remarkably intact. Padre Padilla's body was then clothed in a new robe (the old one having disintegrated) and reburied. The coffin has risen to the surface several times since then. No one has ever quite figured out why (although the area's high water table may provide a clue). Today, however, Padre Padilla rests in peace: during a 1962 renovation of the sanctuary, his grave was covered with concrete.

The Blue Nun

In another strange story, legend has it that in the early days of the mission at Isleta, a large group of Navajo Indians journeyed to Isleta and asked the priest there to baptize them. When asked who had sent them, the Navajos replied that a beautiful young woman dressed in blue robes had told them about Christianity and taught them to pray the rosary. It was she, they said, who told them to find a priest to baptize them into the faith. Around this time, other stories of the lovely "lady in blue" were circulating, especially among the Indians in the southeastern part of the territory.

Who was this mysterious person? Investigation revealed her to be Sister Maria de Jesus Agreda, a Franciscan nun of the Order of St. Clare, who was abbess of her convent in Spain at that time. It seems that Sister Maria was leading a double life: she managed to visit native populations all over the American Southwest without physically leaving her cloister! Sister Maria—who from an early age was prone to visions and religious raptures—was "bi-locating": traveling to the New World in spirit form. Before long, word of the nun and her unusual abilities spread beyond her convent walls. At this time in Spain, the Inquisition was still raging; its officials took a dim view of Sister

Maria's activities. A trial ensued, in the midst of which a group of missionaries returned to Spain from the New World and seemed to confirm the nun's story. Nonetheless, Sister Maria was ordered to cease her controversial missionary work.

There are those who say that it is thanks to Sister Maria of Agreda that so many Native Americans were converted to Catholicism in such a short time. There are others, of course, who say the whole story is ridiculous. What does seem to be true, however, is that Sister Maria of Agreda, who died in 1665, is an "incorruptible": like that of Padre Padilla, her body has never decayed. Her glass-lidded casket lies in a crypt in her monastery; periodic examinations (one made as recently as 1991) have shown that her corpse looks much the same as it did soon after her death.

San Gerónimo, Taos Pueblo

Taos Pueblo

Taos, the northernmost pueblo, is also one of the oldest, with structures more than a thousand years old. Coronado himself never saw Taos, but the reports of his captain, Francisco de Barrio-Nuevo, described a beautiful village with multistoried adobe houses in a most beautiful setting on either side of a fast-running stream—a description that still holds true. Today, Taos Pueblo is one of the most popular tourist destinations in New Mexico. Its dramatic high-rise adobes—set against the background of majestic Taos Mountain—have made it a favorite subject of photographers and artists for centuries.

Throughout New Mexico's early history, Taos was at the center of most rebellions—against the Spanish for most of the seventeenth century and, later (while the rest of the territory seemed to quietly accept the newcomers), against the invading American army in 1846. Reports of unrest surfaced as early as 1609. Don Juan de Oñate, that troublesome first governor of New Mexico, was accused of hurling a young Taos Indian from a rooftop. Already resentful of the tributes demanded by the Spanish, the Indians of Taos were only somewhat pacified by Oñate's removal from

office later that year. Another revolt—quickly quelled—arose in 1613, and another in 1631 in which the resident missionary and the soldiers with him were attacked and slain. After another rebellion in 1640, the pueblo was abandoned by its people for twenty years. It's no wonder that Popé chose Taos as his headquarters when planning the Pueblo Revolt.

Taos Pueblo.

The Taos Uprising

In 1846, the American army, led by General Stephen Watts Kearny, marched into New Mexico. He proclaimed it a territory of the United States in an address shouted from a rooftop on the plaza at Las Vegas, New Mexico, and promised the protection of the U.S. Army to all who submitted to the new government. He also promised swift retribution for any and all who opposed it.

The new government set up headquarters in Santa Fe and, for the most part, the transition from Mexican to American territory was a smooth one. Not so in

The ruins of the church destroyed during the Taos Uprising still stand at Taos Pueblo.

Taos. The Spanish in the nearby towns resented the newcomers and enlisted the Taos Pueblo Indians to aid them in their fight. Charles Bent, the new American governor headquartered at Taos, was killed and scalped in January 1847 along with many other American officials and residents.

The response of the American army was immediate. Although Kearny and most of his troops were headed toward California, a force of more than three hundred soldiers was amassed from the headquarters at Santa Fe and Albuquerque. After battles at Santa Cruz and Embudo, which the Mexicans decisively lost, the American troops marched into Taos, where the remainder of the rebels took refuge in the mission church at Taos Pueblo. The army attacked the church with gun and cannon fire for more than two hours, but the massive adobe walls of San Gerónimo withstood the assault. It wasn't until the next day that the Americans were able to break through the fortress and end the rebellion. The roof of the church was set afire, and shells were thrown into breaches in the adobe created by axes. Finally, enough damage was done to the walls that the cannons were able to break through, and the Mexicans and Taos Indians inside San Gerónimo had no choice but to surrender.

San Gerónimo Church

The first mission church at Taos was built in 1619, and was completely destroyed in the Pueblo Revolt. The second church—built after the reconquest on the same spot—fell at the hands of the U.S. Army. So strong were the walls of that adobe church that the ruins, which watch over the pueblo's cemetery, look very much as they did after the 1847 battle.

The present church, San Gerónimo (St. Jerome), was built in 1850. Also of adobe, it has a single-nave plan with large buttresses in the back. Several traditional features (twin bell towers, an exterior balcony), the white and earth colors of the church exterior and retaining wall, as well as their stair-step design, give San Gerónimo a distinctive look.

San Gerónimo Church, Taos Pueblo.

CHAPTER TWO

Vanished Cities

✝ **Nuestra Señora de los Angeles de Porciúncula de los Pecos, Pecos National Historic Park**

The Village of Five Hundred Warriors

The Pecos Pueblo is long-since abandoned, and all that remains of its great mission church are its red-stone ruins. But in its day, Pecos was the mightiest of all the southwestern pueblos; in fact, with a population of more than two thousand, it was the largest town in what would later become the United States. Situated in the Pecos River Valley about twenty miles southeast of Santa Fe, Pecos had an ideal location: surrounded by timber- and game-filled mountains, running streams, and fertile farmlands, it also had a high piece of ground on which to build the village. The natives called it Cicuye, meaning "village of five hundred warriors"; their people had been living there since AD 1300, though their ancestors started building small settlements in the area at least five hundred years earlier.

The village was built around a central plaza of four- and five-storied buildings with rooftop entrances, reached by ladders that could be pulled inside for safety. A high wall surrounding the village provided fortification and clear views on all sides.

Facing:
The ruins of the 1717 church are now part of the Pecos National Historic Park.

Despite Pecos's dominance over the other pueblos in New Mexico, it was subject to frequent attacks by Apache and Navajo tribes who raided and pillaged Pecos almost as often as they came to trade. And many did come to trade: in addition to all the natural blessings of its surroundings, Pecos's location—surrounded by neighboring pueblos to the north, south, and west, and situated at the gateway to the eastern plains (home to the nomadic hunting tribes)—made it a natural trade center.

Pecos Pueblo has the distinction of having bested Coronado. By the time the conquistador reached Pecos in 1541, still on his quest for gold and riches, some Pecos warriors had returned from a visit to Zuni. Having witnessed the Spaniards' violence there, they knew what to expect—as well as what Coronado was looking for. So the Pecos people welcomed the conquistador and his men, showering them with supplies and regaling them with tales of gold, which, they assured their visitors, could be found farther to the east. They even provided Coronado's party with a guide, a captive Plains tribesman who backed up their stories. Of course, the real plan was to lure the Spanish out into the desolate plains of Kansas where, with any luck, they would all perish. However, only the "guide" died, killed by Coronado once he realized he had been duped. It was the last straw for Coronado, though, and he turned around and headed back to Mexico.

It was the Spanish who named the pueblo Pecos. One story speculates that the name comes from the Spanish word *pecoso* (freckled). A more likely explanation is that Coronado's men were told of the great city while visiting other pueblos, and that the name for Cicuye in the other pueblo's language sounded to the Spanish like "Pecos."

Nuestra Señora de los Angeles de Porciúncula de los Pecos

Don Juan de Oñate visited Pecos within weeks of establishing his headquarters at San Gabriel, no doubt eager to visit the most important pueblo in the territory. One of the ten Franciscans in Oñate's party was sent to Pecos to begin his ministry.

Before 1598 ended, a small chapel was built at Pecos Pueblo. By 1618, however, construction had begun on a much larger church. When Don Pedro de Peralta moved the capital from San Gabriel to Santa Fe in 1610, Pecos Pueblo—so close to the new capital city—became more important than ever. The mission church here reflected that importance: when the church was completed in 1625, it was the largest European structure north of Mexico City. Built of mud and stone, its nave was 150 feet long and forty feet wide, it had six bell towers, and its walls were twenty-two feet thick in places. The church was named Nuestra Señora de los Angeles de Porciúncula: the Mission of Our Lady of the Angels of Porciúncula.

Certainly it was impressive, but it wasn't enough to convince the Pecos people to abandon their own beliefs. Resentment grew when the missionaries smashed and burned the Indians' ceremonial items, and at the demands for tribute from both the Franciscans and the secular officials. Pecos lent its mighty fighting forces to the Pueblo Revolt, and tore the massive church down to its foundations.

A new church was completed in 1717, built over the ruins of the old edifice. This church was much smaller; by that time, the pueblo's population was already in decline.

Not a Bang, But a Whimper

Pecos Pueblo had a difficult time during the years following the revolt. Generations of Spanish occupation and protection had weakened its own once-mighty defenses; the incessant raids of the nearby Plains Indians took a greater toll than ever. The once-proud nation actively welcomed the army of the reconquest in 1692. The new Spanish leader, Don Diego de Vargas, was by all reports a confident and charismatic man who inspired loyalty in all who followed him. More important, his was a benevolent, more tolerant style of leadership: he promised the native people that no more tribute would be exacted by the Spanish, and that the new missionaries he brought with him would be more tolerant of the beliefs of the native people. The Pecos tribe not only submitted to the new regime but also became De Vargas's active allies, sending their own warriors when De Vargas's army marched to reclaim Santa Fe.

The new church was rebuilt on the same spot as the old one. If it was much smaller, the new convento was much larger, with many outbuildings that included stables, schools, and carpentry and weaving shops. The Spanish introduced modern

Pecos church ruins.

tools and building methods, and added wheat and other crops to the traditional corn, beans, and squash. Nonetheless, the decline of the great pueblo continued. Epidemics of smallpox and other European-introduced diseases gradually weakened the population, and Pecos's place as the trade center of the territory was usurped by Santa Fe. By the early 1800s, Pecos Pueblo's population had all but disappeared. In 1838, the last remaining seventeen residents accepted the invitation of their relatives to the north and moved to Jemez Pueblo, where their descendants still reside.

The Great Snake and the Perpetual Fire

Pecos Pueblo had many kivas (underground rooms used for traditional religious ceremonies), and legend has it that in the largest and centermost of these kivas lived a great snake, the protector of the village. The snake was fed with human sacrifices; mothers hid and guarded their children lest they be chosen for the great snake's meal. A fire always burned in this kiva, for the legend held that if the fire went out, the snake would abandon the village and leave it unprotected.

Throughout the years of Spanish occupation, the fire was tended in secret. But as time went by, the population waned and the people grew weaker from the years of famine and disease. Finally, the fire was allowed to die. The era of the great Pecos Pueblo was over.

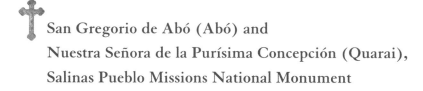

San Gregorio de Abó (Abó) and
Nuestra Señora de la Purísima Concepción (Quarai),
Salinas Pueblo Missions National Monument

The Salinas Pueblos

The area known as the Estancia Basin was a lake several millennia ago. The Spanish called it Salinas (salt beds) because salt—that most valuable and homely of commodities—is what was left behind long after the lake was gone. Located northeast of Socorro in the Manzano Mountains of east-central New Mexico, the area was once home to many thriving Indian villages. All are long gone; what remains today of the three largest—Abó, Quarai, and Gran Quivera (Tabira)—comprise the Salinas National Monument, which has a centrally located visitor center in the town of Mountainair.

The Salinas pueblos seem to be the only native villages spared an encounter with Coronado's exploration parties, although it is speculated that the battle at

Church complex ruins at Quarai.

Hawikuh in Zuni may have spurred immigration into the area. Although there are reports of small exploring parties in the area, no Spaniard seems to have seen the great town of Abó until 1598. In October of that year, Governor Juan de Oñate displayed an early show of strength and control by summoning the influential pueblo leaders and presenting them with the Oath of Obedience to the Spanish Crown, which they were all expected to sign.

Records show that the leaders did indeed sign the oath; however, the pueblos themselves weren't as easily brought into line. In 1600, Spanish soldiers—possibly deserters returning to Mexico City—were attacked near Quarai. Survivors returned north to report the deaths. In a move eerily reminiscent of the disastrous incident at Acoma, Oñate sent his nephew Vicente de Zaldivar to Quarai to retaliate. Zaldivar's party was, in turn, attacked near Abó. In 1601, the Salinas Indians revolted, but they couldn't hold out against the superior firepower of the Spanish. A six-day battle ensued, in which nine hundred Indians were killed, more executed, and still more taken as prisoners or slaves.

Perhaps the Salinas pueblos weren't included in the initial round of mission building because of these incidents. By 1618, though, another group of Franciscans had arrived in New Mexico; by 1622, work was begun on three churches.

These missions were destined to be short lived. In the 1660s, drought came to the Estancia Basin and settled in. The extended dry spell brought even more raids by the Apaches, who were also suffering from its effects. In a 1669 letter, Fray Juan Bernal wrote, "One of the calamities is that the whole land is at war with the heathen Apaches, who kill all the Christian Indians they can find." No crops had been gathered for three years, and the villagers were reduced to eating cowhide blankets and rugs, which they roasted or boiled. People were dying of hunger by the hundreds. Still, it wasn't until 1672 that the food stores hoarded by the priests at Abó— food grown and reaped by the Indians for the mission—were opened to feed the hungry people of the village. By the following year, even those stores were depleted. In 1677, Quarai was abandoned. The next year, those remaining at Abó also left, dispersing northward to other villages. The churches themselves weren't destroyed in

Facing:
The ruins of San
Gregorio de Abó.

the Pueblo Revolt because there was no one left to destroy them. The Indians of the Salinas pueblos never returned to Abó or Quarai.

San Gregorio de Abó

The first church built in the area, San Gregorio de Abó, was begun in 1622. The church was built of dark red sandstone, easily available in the area, and mortared with clay. The style of the walls—small, thin stones held together with earth—is similar to those at Chaco Canyon, the ancestral home of some Pueblo tribes, which had been abandoned long before the Spanish arrived in the New World. Clearly, the Indians knew how to use these stones to build walls. Still, none of them had ever seen a building on this scale: the church's interior was eighty-four feet long

and twenty-five feet wide, with ceilings twenty-five feet high. In a cruciform shape with a clerestory window that magically lit the altar in the mornings, the church must have seemed enormous to those accustomed to much smaller spaces.

In 1640, construction of larger building was initiated by Fray Francisco de Acevedo, one of the most masterful church designers of the early missionaries. His clever design used the old church as a base, and the new edifice was built around it. The result in 1651 was an even larger and grander edifice, complete with a large convento complex with classrooms and workshops. There, the Indians learned to speak Spanish and play European musical instruments, and were instructed in the Christian faith. The ruins at Abó are from this second church, though walls of the first church—incorporated into Acevedo's design—remain as well.

Nuestra Señora de la Purísima Concepción, Quarai

The ruins of Nuestra Señora de la Purísima Concepción (Quarai).

The mission church at Quarai, built around 1628, was even larger than the one at Abó. Like its neighbor, Nuestra Señora de la Purísima Concepción (Our Lady of the

Immaculate Conception) was constructed of the area's abundant red sandstone in a cruciform shape. Both churches had elaborate interiors, with choir lofts and baptisteries, pictures of saints brought from Mexico, and altars lavishly decorated with beautiful vestments, candlesticks, and sacramental vessels.

The Inquisition

In the early days of the seventeenth century, the Spanish Inquisition remained a powerful and greatly feared institution. It first appeared in the new territory in 1613, after an incident involving the territory's second governor, Pedro de Peralta, who, in defiance of an order of the senior Franciscan, sent soldiers from Santa Fe to Taos to collect tribute on a holy day. The priest, Fray Isidro Ordoñez, declared himself an agent of the Inquisition and had Peralta arrested.

For the next sixty years, the Inquisition held sway throughout the territory, especially as conflicts between the civil and religious authorities grew. The Franciscans felt theirs to be the higher authority; the civilians disagreed, especially as the two groups were locked in a heated competition for that most valuable of commodities: the labor of the natives. At Salinas, the rift between the groups was particularly pronounced. In 1660, New Mexico gained a governor, López de Mendizábal, who had little respect for the church. His agent at Salinas, Nicolás de Aguilar, was particularly contemptuous and regularly advised the Indians to disobey the priests. Much to the missionaries' outrage, he allowed the natives to perform their traditional kachina dances, which the Spanish especially enjoyed. The Franciscans, of course, considered the dances satanic and had forbidden them, along with all traditional native practices.

Aguilar even dared to disrupt a church service at Quarai, during which the resident priest was preaching a sermon on obedience to what he considered the highest of authorities: God and the church. Aguilar announced to the astonished congregation that the highest authority in the land was the king, not the church, and it was to the Crown that the pueblo owed its obedience. Aguilar finally was brought before the Inquisition after accusing one of the Franciscans of having an Indian mistress (a charge that appears to have been true). The outraged friar declared that a civil servant had no authority over the clergy, and had him arrested for daring to criticize a priest! Aguilar was later found guilty of many offenses and banished from the territory.

The German Prisoner

Bernardo Gruber was among the last in New Mexico to feel the Inquisition's sting. A German trader from Sonora, Mexio, he spent the winter of 1668 in the Salinas area. On Christmas morning, he attended Mass at Nuestra Señora de la Purísima Concepción church at Quarai. Gruber climbed the ladder to the choir loft and, while the priest preached his Christmas sermon, told the chorus members that he possessed *papelitos* (slips of paper) with magic properties. Anyone who ate one of the papelitos, he said, would be protected from harm for all of that Christmas day.

Soon thereafter, a young man named Juan demonstrated this "magic" to the pueblo elders at the Quarai kiva. After swallowing one of the slips of paper, he stabbed himself repeatedly with a knife. To the astonishment of the others, no blood was drawn. The youth later admitted that it was a trick: he didn't believe the papers had any magic properties and he was only pretending to stab himself, as Gruber had shown him. Still, the damage was done. Bernardo Gruber was arrested and taken to Abó to await trial before the Inquisition.

Gruber went with the ecclesiastical authorities without a struggle. No real harm had been done, after all; he was confident of his eventual exoneration. Unfortunately, the incident took place during troubled times: the period of great drought and fierce raids that would soon lead to the abandonment of the Salinas pueblos had already taken hold. The friars could neither gather the necessary tribunal to try Gruber in New Mexico nor assemble the resources needed to transport him to Mexico City. Still, they refused to release him.

He was imprisoned for more than two years without ever having his case heard. Finally, the German prisoner made plans to escape. Feigning illness, Gruber persuaded his guards to remove his shackles. With the assistance of one of the guards (who owed him money) and a servant from his more prosperous days, Bernardo

Gruber escaped. His taste of freedom was fleeting, however; weeks later, his corpse and that of his horse were found under a tree at the end of the trail called thereafter Jornada del Muerto (Journey of the Dead Man).

Bernardo Gruber's treatment inspired outrage in Mexico City. As a result, the Inquisition's authority in New Mexico was greatly reduced.

The Beloved Priest

In 1650, Fray Gerónimo de la Llana took over the mission at Quarai. He loved the church and the people there; when the good priest died in 1659, he was buried in Nuestra Señora de la Purísima Concepción. The affection was mutual: when Quarai was abandoned in 1677, the Indians insisted that they wouldn't leave the body of their beloved priest behind. They carried him out with them and reinterred his body in a chapel in a nearby town. In 1759, Governor Marín del Valle had the priest's remains taken from the chapel and brought to Santa Fe. Today they are at rest—along with the remains of Fray Asencio de Zárate, the first pastor of the parish church in Santa Fe—in a stone casket in a niche in the Conquistadora Chapel at St. Francis Cathedral.

The stone casket containing the remains of early Franciscans rests in the wall of the Conquistadora Chapel at St. Francis Cathedral in Santa Fe.

CHAPTER THREE

Mud, Wood, and Stone

✠ Building Churches in New Mexico

With a few notable exceptions, most of the oldest buildings in New Mexico are churches. By 1630, there were mission churches at most of the pueblos as well as at least two churches in Santa Fe. That some of these buildings are still standing is a testament to the dedication of the Franciscan missionaries, the building skills of the Pueblo Indians, and the care that has been taken to preserve these churches—never an easy task—throughout the centuries.

Most Franciscans who came to New Mexico in the early days of the territory's settlement had no formal training in architecture, only the rudimentary knowledge gathered during their seminary years in Spain or Mexico. The Crown provided each missionary with a "church kit" containing some basic tools—hoes, axes, saws, nails, and hardware (hinges and latches for the doors)—and what was considered the bare essentials for conducting services: vestments, altar cloths, chalices, bells, candlesticks, missals, containers for holy water, and communion wafers. Replacement items, sent every three years from Mexico on the Camino Real (the Royal Road, the trail between Mexico City and Santa Fe) included beeswax, candle wicks, lamp oil, and soap for washing the vestments and cloths.

Facing:
The beautiful and striking red stonework at Abó and Quarai was originally hidden by layers of mud plaster.

Above:
At Acoma, houses
and other buildings
were traditionally
made of stone. Its
church, however,
was made of adobe:
earth and water
were carried up
to the rock village
in baskets.

Right:
Walls at Zia
Pueblo are made
from cobblestones
and mud.

Labor was provided—not always willingly—by the Pueblo Indians, mostly the women and children as was the custom of the pueblos of that era. But the natives contributed more than just hard work to the task. They also brought their centuries-old knowledge of how to create buildings using the materials available. For example, the ruins at the Salinas pueblos (page 37) display intricate rockwork similar to that at Chaco Canyon, created centuries before any European set foot on the continent.

In areas where stone wasn't as readily available, the Indians made their houses from dried mud. The Spanish themselves were not strangers to adobe. They taught the Indians to make adobe bricks with a centuries-old method thought to have originated in Mesopotamia and been brought to Spain by Arab emigrants. The traditional "puddling" method used by the Indians involved forming mud into low bands that had to be allowed to dry in the sun before another layer could be added on top of it. The brick method was obviously superior—or at least less time-consuming—since many bricks could be quickly made and dried at one time. Using this method, the Spanish were able to construct adobe buildings that were far larger than anything the Indians would ever have dreamed of building.

Mud plaster was applied over the layers of brick, which were sometimes as much as nine feet thick, and was reapplied frequently: buildings of dirt and straw don't take long to return to their elements without constant repair and maintenance.

Early mission churches were usually built using the single-nave plan: one long, narrow space, often with twin bell towers at either end of the façade.

Left:
San Isidro in Sapello
is no longer in use.
The deterioration
of the mud plaster
reveals the adobe
bricks underneath.

Below:
Buttresses like these
at San Gerónimo at
Taos Pueblo were
often employed to
help support the
adobe walls.

The massive church at Acoma Pueblo, a prime example of early mission building, has a single-nave plan with a centered front door and double bell towers. On the far side of the church is the convento, *the priest's residence.*

San José de Gracia at Las Trampas uses the cruciform plan. Note the transept near the back of the church.

Many of the smaller Spanish churches also use this plan, though the shape preferred by the Spanish was the cruciform. Here a transept crosses the nave in front of the sanctuary, forming a cross.

Roofs were constructed by placing large *vigas* (wood beams) across the tops of the walls of the nave. A nave, therefore, could only be as wide as the available roof beams. On top of the vigas were placed either *latillas* (thin sapling branches) or *tablas* (wooden panels), which formed a base for the adobe roof. These roofs were extremely vulnerable to weather and the passage of time, and needed to be repaired and even replaced often. Many New Mexico churches that once had flat roofs now have roofs of pitched metal.

Inside, the heavy vigas were often supported by *corbels* (carved wooden corner pieces), which were decorative as well as practical. The ceiling over the sanctuary usually was made higher than that of the nave. The difference in space made possible the transverse clerestory window that, though hidden from the nave, bathed the sanctuary in a mystical morning light.

This old Spanish church—beautifully decorated with santero art—*has a ceiling of exposed* vigas *supported by carved corbels.*

This smaller church doesn't need corbels to support its vigas.

Note: The Archdiocese of Santa Fe has requested that interiors of the small churches not be identified by location.

At Cristo Rey Church in Santa Fe, light from the clerestory window bathes the magnificent stone altar screen in morning sunlight. Note also the latillas *over the* vigas.

PART TWO

The Wild West

CHAPTER ONE

North— Sangre de Cristo

✝ ## Santa Cruz de la Cañada, Santa Cruz

The tiny settlement of Santa Cruz was originally occupied by early colonists who had either fled or been killed during the Pueblo Revolt. After peace was reestablished and new settlers began pouring into Santa Fe, it soon became apparent that the capital was woefully inadequate to accommodate all the new colonists. Governor Diego de Vargas realized that another town—a Spanish town—would be necessary. Santa Cruz, some twenty-five miles north in the foothills of the Sangre de Cristo Mountains, seemed an ideal solution. In the years following the revolt, however, local Indians had taken up residence in their abandoned houses. De Vargas forced them to return to their pueblos and then ordered all nonmilitary settlers to leave the overcrowded capital and make their homes in the new town, which he named La Villa Nueva de Santa Cruz de los Españoles Mejicanos del Rey Nuestro Señor Carlos Segundo (The New City of the Holy Cross of the Mexican Spaniards of Our Lord the King Charles II). Not surprisingly, the town rather quickly became known as Santa Cruz de la Cañada (Holy Cross of the Narrow Valley)—and eventually, just Santa Cruz.

Facing:
Santa Cruz
de la Cañada,
Santa Cruz.

A small church was built at Santa Cruz right away. In 1733, construction began on the present church, one of the most impressive and well preserved in New Mexico. Completed in 1743, the large adobe church was built in the cruciform shape, with huge buttresses and double bell towers topped with crosses. A third cross perches at the peak of the pitched roof, which was added in the early 1900s to protect the church and its magnificent artwork against damage from rain and snow.

The church today is beautifully maintained and is a stunning example of early Spanish Colonial architecture. The interior is no less impressive: oil paintings sent by the Spanish Crown during the earliest years of colonization share space with *bultos* (statues), *reredos* (altar screens), and *retablos* (paintings on wood) by New Mexican *santeros* (artists who created *santos* [holy images]) that date back to the 1700s.

The Statue's Missing Fingers

Among the many beautiful bultos at Santa Cruz de la Cañada is a statue of El Jésus Nazareno—Jesus of Nazareth. Legend has it that one spring, a great storm in the mountains caused the Santa Cruz River to rise up, putting the town and church in danger. One of the fingers was cut from the wooden statue and thrown into the river. Miraculously, the storm abated, the floodwaters receded, and the town was saved.

A few years later, another of El Jésus Nazareno's fingers was sacrificed, this time during a terrible outbreak of smallpox. This time the wooden digit was burned and its ashes mixed with those of the palm branches for the Ash Wednesday services. The story says that those who were anointed with these ashes did not fall ill.

✝ The High Road to Taos

New settlers from Mexico and Spain continued to arrive in New Mexico, lured by the promise of land grants to new colonists. By the middle of the eighteenth century, small farming communities began springing up in the fertile mountain lands between Santa Fe and Taos. It wasn't an easy life, but despite many hardships—a short growing season, hard winters, and continued attacks from the Apaches, Navajos, and the fierce Comanches (another nomadic tribe that had recently arrived in the area)—these remote villages persevered.

Churches at Santa Cruz and nearby Picurís Pueblo were already in place, but as the communities grew, so did the desire for churches of their own. By the late 1700s, however, the Franciscans had lost much of their authority in New Mexico. Many left their missions and returned to Mexico. They were replaced by lay clergy, priests who were not affiliated with an order (such as the Franciscans). More importantly, these secular priests were not employed by the Spanish Crown. The churches in these small communities were not funded by the king; the people of the villages had to finance the building of their churches themselves. Perhaps this is one reason that these churches—much smaller and more humbly built than some of the grand Crown-sponsored missions—have a unique charm that reflects their communities, and have been so devotedly cared for and preserved by them over the centuries. Many of these small churches, located on or near what is called the "High Road to Taos" (one of the loveliest and most popular scenic byways anywhere), are home to exquisite examples of santero art: bultos, reredos, and retablos, lovingly crafted by santeros to decorate the churches they worked so hard to build.

San José de Gracia de las Trampas, Las Trampas

One of the first of these rural settlements was at Las Trampas (The Traps), probably named for the snares used by local fur traders. Founded in 1754 by a retired soldier from Santa Fe and twelve other families, the village petitioned the Bishop of Durango for a church of their own during his visit in 1760. The petition was granted, but the villagers had to raise the money themselves (each family giving a portion of their meager income every year), and the church, San José de Gracia de las Trampas (St. Joseph of Grace of las Trampas), was not completed until 1776. It was worth the wait: the church is a beautiful example of Spanish Colonial architecture, with many of the features that make the historic churches of New Mexico so unique. Built of

*San José de Gracia
de las Trampas,
Las Trampas.*

adobe in the cruciform shape, it has a clerestory window, double bell towers to which wooden belfries were added, and an exterior balcony that was likely used by the choir or as an exterior pulpit during the processions and fiestas that took place outside the church. Its interior has a wood floor and carved wooden choir loft and altar rail; even today, it is lit only by sunlight or with candles. Gorgeous retablos decorate the walls of the nave, and the reredos in San José de Gracia de las Trampas are perhaps the most dramatic and colorful of all the santero altar screens.

Nuestra Señora del Sagrado Rosario, Truchas

The village of Truchas (Trout) was founded a few years after Las Trampas by another twelve families from the Santa Cruz–Chimayó area. Literally perched at the edge of a canyon, this beautiful little village looks much the same today as it must have years ago, with its narrow roads, tiny adobe houses, and spectacular views of the Sangre de Cristo Mountains. Its church, Nuestra Señora del Sagrado

Nuestra Señora del Sagrado Rosario, Truchas.

Rosario (Our Lady of the Rosary) was not built until 1805, probably because of financial concerns. Before then, the Truchas settlers journeyed to Las Trampas to attend services, literally risking their lives to do so: on at least one occasion, worshippers were attacked and killed by Comanches on their way to Sunday Mass. The church at Truchas is smaller and plainer than its cousin at Las Trampas, but is no less charming. It has a single bell tower and pitched roof (with metal paneling added around 1900). It too is home to santero artwork.

San Antonio de Padua, Córdova

San Antonio de Padua, Córdova.

Other area villages had the benefit of a patron. San Antonio de Padua (St. Anthony of Padua) in Córdova, tucked off the road on a tiny plaza, was built in

Nuestra Señora de San Juan de los Lagos, Talpa.

1830 by wealthy patron Don Bernardo Abeyta, who also built the *santuario* at Chimayó. The tiny town of Córdova is particularly known for its families of wood-workers who have been creating *bultos* and other carvings for generations.

Nuestra Señora de San Juan de los Lagos, Talpa

The church at Talpa, near the very end of the High Road, was financed by a well-to-do member of the community, Don Bernardo Durán, who wanted a chapel for his little village despite its proximity to the grand edifice of San Francisco de Asís in nearby Ranchos de Taos. Built in 1828, the graceful rounded façade of Nuestra Señora de San Juan de los Lagos (Our Lady of St. John of the Lakes) supports three wooden crosses, two smaller ones at either corner, and a larger one over the bell tower at the center. Both the Talpa church and San Antonio in Córdova contain fine examples of *santero* art.

Sangre de Cristo, Cuarteles

San Juan Nepomuceno, Llano San Juan

All over New Mexico are smaller churches for smaller communities. Two charming examples in this area are the 1849 Sangre de Cristo (Blood of Christ) church in Cuarteles, on the road between Chimayó and Santa Cruz, and the 1832 church of San Juan Nepomuceno (St. John Nepomuceno), a short distance off the High Road in the tiny farming hamlet of Llano San Juan.

Nuestra Señora de Guadalupe, Velarde

A larger church served Velarde, a nearby town in the Rio Grande Valley north of Española. Like many of its neighbors up on the High Road, it was settled in the mid-eighteenth century; its fertile land has been primarily known for its apple orchards. Velarde's church, Nuestra Señora de Guadalupe (Our Lady of Guadalupe), was built in 1817 and has thick adobe walls, rear buttresses, and a wooden bell tower atop its pitched roof. A lovely circular stained glass window sits just above the church's wooden front door.

Nuestra Señora de Guadalupe, Velarde.

Santuario de Chimayó, Chimayó

No other church in New Mexico is as famous, as venerated, and as visited as the small adobe chapel in the remote village of Chimayó. Each year on Good Friday, thousands of pilgrims journey on foot to the shrine known as the "Lourdes of the Southwest." Some walk only a mile or two; many others cover the thirty-five miles from Santa Fe; still others walk all the way from Albuquerque (eighty-five miles) or even farther. Visitors come all through the year as well, some drawn by the beauty and serenity of the little chapel and its setting, others in search of healing. Almost everyone takes home some of the "holy dirt" for which the santuario is famous.

Chimayó was first settled by the Spanish in the very early 1700s. Here, family groups built several small enclaves around enclosed plazas in the area. Over the years, the community grew and became known for its abundant crops of apricots and apples, as well as for the beautiful weavings done by local artisans. In one of these enclaves, El Potrero, lived the prosperous and devout Abeyta family.

Santuario de Chimayó.

Don Bernardo's crucifix: Our Lord of Esquipulas.

The Miraculous Crucifix

On Good Friday of the year 1810, Don Bernardo Abeyta was performing his prayers and penances on a hillside near El Potrero when he noticed a bright light shining in the distance. Coming closer, he saw that the light was illuminating a spot near the bank of the Santa Cruz River. There in the ground he found a large wooden crucifix, an image he called "Our Lord of Esquipulas," after the shrine in Guatemala to which his ancestors had long been devoted. He immediately called his neighbors to admire and venerate his find. A small party was dispatched to Santa Cruz to tell the priest there about Don Bernardo's discovery. Good Friday services had just ended; the entire congregation followed them back to Chimayó. The crucifix was then carried with great ceremony back to Santa Cruz and given a place of honor in a niche in the altar.

The next morning, the crucifix was gone. It reappeared in Chimayó at the same place Don Bernardo had found it. Again it was taken to Santa Cruz and again it disappeared, only to reappear in Chimayó. After the third such incident, Don Bernardo decided to build a small chapel next to his house to shelter the crucifix, which clearly wanted to remain in Chimayó.

In another version of this story, the crucifix belonged to a Guatemalan priest who had wandered the area many years earlier and who was believed to have been killed by Indians. A flood that spring washed up the crucifix (and, in some versions, the priest's body), which old-timers recognized as belonging to the priest from Esquipulas. Yet another legend says that the crucifix came to the church after it had already been built, brought in a wooden box by a donkey that seemed to appear out of nowhere and was found waiting at the door to the church.

In still other versions, the finding of the crucifix and the first healings at the site happened much earlier, to ancestors of some of the villagers.

What does seem beyond dispute is that the spot where the crucifix was supposedly found had long been sacred ground to the Tewa Indians who lived in the area well before the arrival of the Spanish, and who had always recognized the dirt's healing properties. It's also true that in 1813, Don Bernardo Abeyta asked permission to build a larger chapel at El Potrero so that the pilgrims flocking to the area could more easily seek healing and honor Our Lord of Esquipulas.

The Santuario

Permission was granted and the church was constructed over the next three years. It was built in the colonial style, with thick adobe walls and customary double bell towers, but with a simple, single-nave construction. It is surrounded by an adobe wall; even more than most, its open gateway seems to welcome its visitors.

Don Bernardo himself commissioned the most prominent santeros of the day to create art for his chapel. The result of his generosity is the treasure trove of bultos and retablos that grace the chapel, with the crucifix of Our Lord of Esquipulas in the prominent place in the center of the altar screen.

Pilgrims come from around the world to gather "holy dirt" from this hole in the floor at Chimayó.

To the left of the sanctuary, a low doorway leads to a side chapel filled with small shrines and pictures as well as a collection of crutches and braces and other artifacts of illness left behind by those cured at Chimayó. At the back of this chapel, through another low doorway, is the tiny room with a hole in its floor—El Pocito—which marks the spot where the crucifix was discovered by Don Bernardo, and where pilgrims and tourists collect the "holy dirt" that is said to have effected many miraculous cures.

✝ San Francisco de Asís, Ranchos de Taos

San Francisco de Asís in Ranchos de Taos is one of the most photographed churches in the world. Certainly it is beautiful: a huge cruciform-plan adobe church with double bell towers, an arched doorway, and a square-gated wall around the front. But what makes it so irresistible to photographers and artists is not its lovely façade but the enormous adobe buttresses at the back and sides of the church, across which shadows play and change in the afternoon light. Some say that at a certain time of day during certain times of the year, the face of Jesus appears in the shadows.

In the years following the reconquest, the area around Taos was particularly vulnerable to attacks by the nomadic Comanche tribe—a new threat on the New Mexico frontier—and for many years all the settlers in the area gathered at Taos Pueblo for protection. In 1779, a treaty was reached with the Comanches, and tentative resettlement of outlying villages began. That year, a plaza was built in the village south of Taos. Originally called Las Trampas de Taos, it was also known as El Puestro (The

San Francisco de Asís, Ranchos de Taos.

Outpost) and eventually El Rancho, and had long been dedicated to St. Francis of Assisi. Still, the village did not build its church for another twenty years, probably because raids by the Comanches and other Plains tribes were still very much a problem despite the treaty. Eventually, as these threats subsided, work began on the church; San Francisco de Asís was completed in 1810.

In 1821, Mexico achieved its independence from Spain. This meant the end of trade restrictions (which had been the cause of much strife) between New Mexico and the American and French traders who had long been trying to get into the territory. Suddenly, foreign goods—and foreigner traders and settlers—began pouring into the area. Twenty-five years later, the United States claimed New Mexico (which included the former Spanish lands all the way to California) for its own. The American conquest was a nonevent in most of New Mexico. In Santa Fe, Governor Manuel Armijo fled the territory without a fight, turning the capital over to General Stephen Watts Kearny. In Taos, however, the Hispanic settlers joined with local Indians and with settlers from nearby Mora to launch an ill-fated rebellion, which

The rear buttresses, San Francisco de Asís, Ranchos de Taos.

resulted in the death of the first American-appointed governor, Charles Bent, the destruction of San Gerónimo church at Taos Pueblo, and the absolute leveling of the town of Mora. More change was soon to come when the Vatican created the Vicariate of Santa Fe. New Mexico's clergy, previously under the auspices of the Bishop of Durango in Mexico, had long been used to the independence that comes from being far from the eyes of authority. That freedom came to an abrupt end with the arrival of Bishop Jean Baptiste Lamy.

San Francisco de Asís church survived all these changes. Many beautiful examples of old Spanish and New Mexican santero art decorate the church's interior, which today is still an active parish as well as a popular stop for tourists.

The Controversial Priest and the Mountain Man

Padre José Martínez served the people of Taos as its priest through the many changes of the nineteenth century. Born in Abiquiú, Martínez became a priest later in life after the death of his young wife. A great believer in education, Padre Martínez founded Taos's first coeducational school for children. He also brought a printing press to Taos and printed schoolbooks and religious tracts as well as the town's first newspaper.

In the days following Mexico's declaration of independence from Spain, Taos was suddenly open to an influx of foreign traders. Among them was the most famous of American mountain men, Kit Carson, who arrived in Taos in 1826. He was baptized a Catholic by Padre Martínez in order to marry a local girl, Josefa Jaramillo.

These two prominent citizens of Taos became enemies after the Taos Uprising of 1847. Martínez had been accused of being one of the instigators of the rebellion, a charge that has never been proved. Carson believed it, however. As an American—and as a man who lost family in the uprising—he never forgave Martínez. Willa Cather's *Death Comes for the Archbishop* paints Padre Martínez in the worst possible light, as corrupt and unorthodox and definitely guilty of not only instigating the uprising but of profiting from the event. Her book, of course, is told from the point of view of the new archbishop, Jean Baptiste Lamy (called Latour in the book), who clashed with Padre Martínez almost immediately after Lamy's arrival in New Mexico. Lamy had Martínez removed from his parish and excommunicated. From all accounts, Padre Martínez ignored these edicts and continued to minister to his flock (albeit without official sanction) until his death in 1867.

☦ Santo Tomás Apóstol and Santa Rosa de Lima, Abiquiú

The town of Abiquiú is most famous as the home of artist Georgia O'Keeffe, who lived and painted here for many years until her death in 1986. It's not hard to understand the attraction: in addition to the wide blue skies, mountain views, and magical high desert light that has always attracted visual artists—and which most of northern New Mexico can claim—the landscape around Abiquiú boasts outrageous and otherworldly red rock formations that make it unique in this most unique of lands.

The history of Abiquiú begins much like that of many of the older pueblo settlements, with emigration from the Four Corners area near Farmington, New Mexico. But there the similarities end: the area had already been abandoned by the time the Spanish arrived in 1598, and no Spanish settlements were attempted here before the Pueblo Revolt. Even after the reconquest, settlements were slow to appear and rarely took hold. The Chama Valley had long been Apache territory; to make matters worse, the Comanche and Ute tribes joined forces in the late 1600s to overtake the region.

It wasn't until the 1730s that small settlements were seriously attempted. The first church was built at Santa Rosa de Lima de Abiquiú in the 1740s, but the entire settlement was abandoned in 1747 following a devastating Ute-Comanche raid in which all the women and children were either killed or taken captive.

In 1750, the governor forced the settlers to move back to their villages or lose the titles to their lands. Abiquiú was the northwesternmost outpost of Spanish territory; these outlying settlements provided a much-needed buffer against Indian raids between the northern wilderness and the larger Spanish settlements farther

The ruins of the second church of Santa Rosa de Lima still stand in the valley below Abiquiú.

south. To somewhat lessen the isolation of the returning colonists, the governor sent along a group of Indians known as Genízaros. These were people of mixed tribal descent, primarily the descendants of Plains Indians who had been captured and ransomed by the Spanish. These Hispanicized Indians were given their own land grant (the first such grant for non-Pueblo Indians) at the old mesa-top village that is now considered the heart of Abiquiú. The Santa Rosa settlement was in the valley below on the banks of the Rio Chama. A new church, dedicated to Santa Rosa de Lima, was built there, but the Santa Rosa settlers often took refuge from raids in the Genízaro village.

The church on the Abiquiú plaza, Santo Tomás Apóstol (St. Thomas the Apostle), was not completed until 1772. This church burned down in 1867 and was rebuilt by the villagers. The beautiful church now on the Abiquiú plaza was designed by architect John Gaw Meem in 1930. Meem and his Society for the Preservation of New Mexico Mission Churches helped provide the people of Abiquiú, who made the adobe bricks and built the church themselves, with the means to create a church that honors the best of the old New Mexico style.

The Witches of Abiquiú

In the early days of the Genízaro settlement at Abiquiú, a terrible sickness swept through the pueblo. When the priest fell ill and later died, witchcraft was rumored to be the cause. The Genízaros, who had lived among the Spanish for generations, were considered to be Christian, but in fact most continued to practice the rites and ceremonies of their native traditions. When Abiquiú's new priest, Fray Juan José Toledo, also fell ill, he launched an investigation against suspected witches in the community.

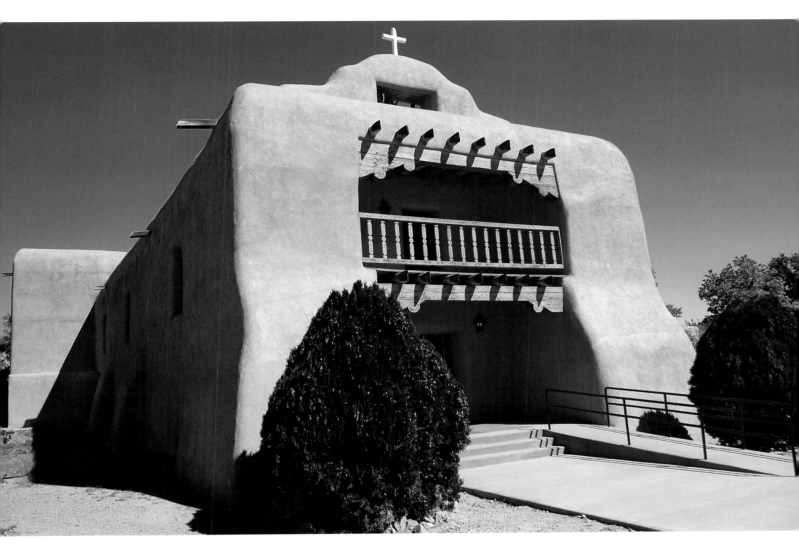

Santo Tomás Apóstol, Abiquiú.

Fifteen people were arrested and imprisoned, but the primary suspect behind the sickness was an admitted *brujo* (folk magician or witch) named El Cojo. He too was arrested and whipped on the Abiquiú plaza, but not until he was threatened with being burned at the stake did he surrender the idols, rattles, and other items considered demonic by the priests. What followed was a systematic destruction of native spiritual objects and sites that had not been seen since the days before the Pueblo Revolt. Ironically, several of the other "witches" died from the very illness they were accused of causing. Incidents of demonism and subsequent trials persisted until 1766.

✝ The Penitente Brotherhood

Los Hermanos de la Fraternidad Piados de Nuestra Padre Jesús Nazareno (The Brothers of the Pious Fraternity of Our Father Jesus the Nazarene), more commonly known as Los Hermanos or the Penitentes, have been a presence in New Mexico's religious life since the early nineteenth century. However, the roots of their most famous practice—self-flagellation—date back much earlier to the disciplinary practices of some European orders in the Middle Ages. Flagellation was in common practice in the earliest New Mexico colonies; it is referred to in passing in a 1620 letter by Fray Alonso de Benavides.

Morada *near Abiquiú.*

Male members of the early colonies, accompanied as they were by Franciscan clergy, were usually members of the Third Order of Saint Francis, a lay order that believed the virtues of asceticism and humility should be adopted not only by Franciscan friars and priests but by ordinary men as well. The num-

ber of Franciscans dwindled, however, as the colonial period drew to an end. After Mexican independence was declared, the rest left the territory. Around that time, Los Hermanos chose to distance themselves from the Franciscans, whose work had been funded by the Spanish Crown, and to adopt the new name for their society.

Even before the loss of the Franciscans, the territory's more remote communities often had been without any priests at all. Into this void stepped Los Hermanos who, in addition to giving both temporal and spiritual guidance to their communities, also presided over baptisms, weddings, and funerals. For more than twenty years, the Brotherhood provided most of the spiritual leadership in the towns of northern New Mexico.

Los Hermanos came into conflict with the new regime ushered in under Bishop Lamy, who naturally expected the local faithful to submit to his authority and to the spiritual leadership provided by the priests he brought with him from Europe. The new bishop was appalled at the disciplinary practices of the Brotherhood and ordered them to cease. Instead, the Penitentes went underground. For more than one hundred years their rituals and ceremonies have been practiced in the utmost secrecy in secluded *moradas* (plain, often windowless buildings).

The rite of self-flagellation was usually performed during Holy Week— sometimes privately, sometimes in processions—accompanied by chanting and singing. The implement used was made from the braided ropes of the yucca plant, with a knot at the end of the braid. The *hermano* struck himself over one shoulder, then the other, hitting the same spot over and over. The drawing of blood was facilitated by the open wound in the shape of a cross that each hermano bore on his back, the mark of his initiation into the Brotherhood. The wound was reopened each Lent and kept open until Easter Sunday. On Good Friday, the processions often culminated in reenactments of the crucifixion.

In recent years, the chasm between the Catholic Church and Los Hermanos has healed, and although many of their rituals are still shrouded in mystery, they have come out somewhat from the shadows. Crucifixion reenactments are still performed

Many moradas
use this sculpture of
Christ bearing the cross.

privately (with more moderate guidelines than in days past), but men carrying crosses on the Good Friday pilgrimages to Chimayó are a common sight.

In his book *My Penitente Land*, Fray Angelico Chavez talks about the "peculiarly universal Hispanic preoccupation with the material cross on which Christ had bled and died" and the act of self-flagellation as "the Spanish soul at its most fervent." This fascination and identification with the suffering Christ is also reflected in the crucifixes fashioned by the santeros of the eighteenth and nineteenth centuries. Unlike more sanitized versions of the crucifixion, the New Mexican figures are bloody and even gory, clearly in agony.

There are still Penitente moradas in most northern New Mexico towns, many in plain view by the roadside and marked by large wooden sculptures of

Christ bearing the cross. If there aren't quite as many members today as there were one hundred years ago, there are still plenty. Los Hermanos are considered now—as then—to be influential community leaders who have committed to an austere and humble path.

The Crypto-Jews

It has been speculated that the origins of the Penitentes are hidden in the mysteries preserved by the Crypto-Jews who came to the New World in the sixteenth century. In the Middle Ages, Jews were expelled from many European countries; many fled to Spain. Most of these converted, some sincerely, many more to escape anti-Semitism while secretly preserving the beliefs and rituals of their forefathers. These were the Crypto-Jews.

Penitente-style crucifix.

Having driven the Moors out of Spain by 1492, Ferdinand and Isabella announced that all Jews would be expelled from the land as well. Even those who had converted were targeted for persecution by the Spanish Inquisition. Many joined expeditions to the New World. Even in New Spain, though, Jews—converted or otherwise—were subject to the Inquisition, so it was expedient to keep their origins a secret. It's possible that these secret Jews embraced the most excessive disciplinary practices to prove just how very "Christian" they were. In New Mexico today, there are families who trace their ancestry back to the early colonists, who also retain family traditions of lighting candles on Friday night, who avoid pork, and who play a game with a wooden top that very much resembles a dreidel. Some of these same families have strong roots in the Penitente Brotherhood.

CHAPTER TWO

Santos and Santeros

✝ Sacred Decorations in New Mexico Churches

In the Spanish Catholic imagination, a church not decorated with images of Christ and the saints is a poor church indeed. As the missions became more established, sacred images in the forms of statues and paintings were brought on the supply wagons that traveled the Camino Real. These early works—most of which no longer exist—likely were used by Franciscans and artists from the community as models from which to create their own church decorations.

The santero period began in the mid-1700s and continued through the late nineteenth century. The work of the artists of that period is the art for which New Mexico churches are justifiably famous. The images (*santos*) made by *santeros* are generally one of three types: *reredos* (altar screens), *retablos* (paintings on wood), or *bultos* (statues).

Reredos

New Mexico churches are perhaps best known for their magnificent reredos. These altar screens are painted panels set into an architectural frame. The panels usually

Facing:
Very few pieces from before the Pueblo Revolt still exist. This image of San Miguel, painted on animal hide in the 1630s, is believed to be the work of a Franciscan friar.

These two reredos are the work of Raphael Aragón, one of the most prolific nineteenth-century santeros.

RESTAURACION HECHA
EN 1975 POR LA COFRADIA
DE LA CONQUISTADORA
CON FONDOS DEL
MONSEÑOR TRUST

PINTADA POR
PEDRO ANTONIO FRESQUIS
1809

display images of saints and angels; sometimes a bulto is placed in a *nicho* (recessed shelf) in the screen. Reredos are used not only behind the altar in the main sanctuary but also to decorate the side chapels created by the transepts in cruciform-plan churches.

The beautiful reredos with its famous image of Our Lady of Guadalupe (see page 121) is not the work of a New Mexico santero but was brought from Mexico on the Camino Real. One of the first screens done locally is the magnificent stone reredos now displayed at Cristo Rey Church in Santa Fe (see page 137). Thought (though not known) to be the work of the santero Bernardo Miera y Pacheco, the stone screen may be the model that inspired many other locally created reredos.

Because of the nature and intention of these sacred decorations, the identities of the individual artists were not thought to be important at the time the art was made. Some works, however, were signed or otherwise identified by the artist. Today, the identities of many of the santeros are known and their works identified.

Facing and below: This altar screen, whose center nicho now holds a retablo of La Conquistadora by another artist, was signed by santero Pedro Antonio Frequis.

Right:
This small
reredos *is also
the work of Pedro
Antonio Frequis.*

Facing:
*This brightly
painted altar
screen was built
in the early
1800s. In 1860,
it was painted
over with these
images by José de
Gracia Gonzales.
The* bultos *are
probably the
work of Bernardo
Miera y Pacheco.*

Facing:
The wide reredos *at this small church is by an unknown* santero.

Left:
Don Bernardo Abeyta commissioned José Aragón to make this altar screen for his chapel. The bulto *in the lower center nicho is of the archangel San Raphael and was carved by Raphael Aragón. The image of God the Father looks down from the top panel.*

Right:
This reredos, *also by José Aragón, includes an image of Our Lady of Guadalupe and a large* bulto *of Jésus Nazareno clad in a purple robe.*

Facing:
This modern altar screen is the work of Robert Lentz. Installed at St. Francis Cathedral in 1986 as part of the cathedral's centennial rededication, the reredos *celebrates the Saints of the Americas. In the center* nicho *is a statue of St. Francis from Santa Fe's 1717* parróquia *(parish church).*

Retablos

A retablo is a painting done on a flat surface, usually a pine board that has been hand-adzed and covered with gesso before being painted.

Stations of the Cross

Most Catholic churches contain a set of fourteen retablos known as Stations of the Cross. The devotion—a series of prayers said as participants retrace the steps of Jesus from his arrest to his death on the cross—was begun by St. Francis of Assisi.

Above right:
Painted by José de Gracia
Gonzales in the mid-1800s,
this retablo *depicts Our*
Lady of Carmel, the hope of
the souls in Purgatory.

Right:
The Holy Trinity is featured
in this retablo, *also by*
José de Gracia Gonzales.

Facing:
Raphael Aragón painted
this retablo *of the Madonna*
and Child in 1862.

Right:
This Station of the
Cross, which shows
Veronica wiping
the face of Jesus,
is an oil painting
from Mexico.

Facing:
This retablo, *which*
also depicts the
encounter between
Jesus and Veronica,
was one of the
Stations of the Cross
that was mass-
produced in
Durango, Mexico,
in the late nine-
teenth century. Sets
like these are found
in many New
Mexico churches.
As the bright colors
here attest, this
particular set was
recently cleaned
and restored.

This Station of
the Cross is not
a retablo *but a
molded sculpture.
Made from com-
pressed marble dust
that has been fired
and painted to look
like carved marble,
this is one of the set
brought from Italy
to grace the Loretto
Chapel in Santa Fe.*

In 1975, a fifteenth Station of the Cross depicting the Resurrection of Christ was approved by Pope Paul VI.

Marie Romero Cash, a local san-tera, *was commissioned in 1997 by Archbishop Michael Sheehan to create these beautiful* santero-*style Stations of the Cross for St. Francis Cathedral. Returning* santero-*style art to the cathedral built by Archbishop Jean Baptiste Lamy, under whose watch the* santero *works fell out of favor (and were in many cases painted over or destroyed), seems a fitting reconciliation.*

Bultos

A *bulto* is a *santo* in the round, usually carved from a cottonwood root.

These two small bultos of St. Joseph and the Virgin Mary are placed next to their counterparts on the altar screen behind them. These statues, made by an unknown artist, are not bultos a vestir (statues meant to be dressed) but are clothed to protect them from further deterioration.

Below left: This bulto of St. Francis of Assisi was probably the work of the artist known only as the Laguna Santero. The statue stands in the nicho of an altar screen by the same artist.

Far right: The most famous bulto of all is La Conquistadora, the oldest Madonna figure in the New World. First brought to Santa Fe in 1625 by Fray Alonzo de Benavides, the statue returned to New Mexico with Don Diego de Vargas after the Pueblo Revolt.

Crucifixes

Above left:
Penitente-style Cristos *(Christ figures) populate most northern New Mexico churches. This hand-carved folk-art piece graphically illustrates the suffering of the crucified Christ.*

Above center:
Even older churches sometimes use more conventional church art. This crucifix is displayed in one of the southern pueblo churches.

Above right:
This colorful Cristo retablo *is probably by José de Gracia Gonzales.*

Cristos *are often placed in nichos in altar screens. The one on the left is by Raphael Aragón; on the right are a* Cristo *and two* bultos *in a* reredos *by the* santero *Molleno.*

CHAPTER THREE

South—
Camino Real

✝ San Felipe de Neri, Albuquerque

Albuquerque—New Mexico's largest city—got off to a rather rough start in life, founded as it was in an act of political obsequiousness by an upstart who grabbed his chance to leave a lasting mark. When Governor De Vargas died in 1704, the interim governor—one Don Francisco Curvo y Valdez—decided to make his short stay in office count. Certainly there was a need for another town—the colony of New Mexico was growing rapidly in the years following the reconquest. The interim governor sent some thirty settlers to an area along the Rio Grande fifty miles south of Santa Fe and just north of Isleta Pueblo. He named the town San Francisco de Alburquerque for his own patron saint and for his Spanish patron, the Duke of Alburquerque. That worthy, however, was far from pleased at the presumption of Don Francisco, who had no authority as a temporary official to found a city. The duke immediately renamed the city after the king's patron saint; thus, the town became known as San Felipe de Alburquerque. Don Francisco was reprimanded and removed from his office. Despite its bad beginning, though, the town he founded prospered.

Facing:
San Felipe de Neri,
Albuquerque.

The first church here was built the same year as the city's founding—1706—on the west side of the plaza in what is now Albuquerque Old Town (the extra "r" in the duke's title was dropped from the town's name sometime later). Named San Felipe de Neri (St. Philip Neri), it was by all accounts a lovely church. By the end of the eighteenth century, however, it was falling into disrepair; it collapsed in 1792 after a severe rainstorm. Construction on a new church on the north side of the plaza was begun almost immediately. The large adobe church is in the Spanish Colonial style and has a cruciform shape. The twin bell towers that were added in 1861 by Father Joseph Machebeuf (who came to New Mexico with Bishop Jean Baptiste Lamy and was later named the first bishop of Denver) reflect the more Romanesque style favored by the French priests of the era. Today, San Felipe de Neri remains an important and thriving parish.

Military Maneuvers

General Stephen Watts Kearny marched into Albuquerque and claimed it for the United States in 1846, two years before the Treaty of Guadalupe Hidalgo would make that claim official. Sixteen years later, Albuquerque was briefly occupied during the Civil War by Confederate soldiers, who made their headquarters on the Old Town Plaza across from San Felipe de Neri Church. The Confederates retreated after their decisive defeat at Glorieta, and Albuquerque was once again under Union control.

The "Sorrowful" Priest

Church baptismal records seem to give credence to the story about a parish priest with a great devotion to the Virgin Mary in her role as Our Lady of Sorrows (Nuestra Señora de los Dolores). During his long tenure at San Felipe de Neri, every child the good priest baptized, male and female, was given the name of Dolores. Happily, it does seem this sorrowful (though lovely) appellation was tagged on to each child's other given names.

✝ San Miguel Mission, Socorro

Some say that the first church in New Mexico was not at Ohkay Owingeh (San Juan Pueblo), but here, where Don Juan de Oñate's party of future colonists stopped in 1598 on their way north. The Indians at the village of Pilabo gave the weary travelers a generous—and much needed—gift of corn; Oñate promptly renamed the village Soccoro (Help) and in gratitude left behind two Franciscan priests, who may well have built a small chapel here before Oñate had a chance to settle in at San Juan Pueblo. A much larger and more impressive mission church, Nuestra Señora de Perpetua Socorro (Our Lady of Perpetual Help), with thick adobe walls and huge roof beams harvested from the nearby mountains, was completed in 1626. The mission at Socorro was one of the more successful. When the Pueblo Revolt came in 1680, the Indians here did not participate but fled with the Spanish to El Paso del Norte. After the reconquest, the Pilabo Indians did not return to their former home but remained south in the new village they had established in what is now Texas, Socorro del Sur (Socorro of the South).

Socorro remained empty, its mission abandoned, for more than one hundred years—until around 1800, when Spanish and Mexican settlers began to rebuild. The church had been badly damaged in the revolt and suffered (as adobe always will) from the many years of neglect. Yet the thick walls and massive beams still stood and the new church—dedicated as San Miguel and completed in 1821—was rebuilt using the old one as a foundation. The first church had originally been constructed in the Spanish Colonial style, but this reconstruction and subsequent renovations have altered its original appearance. Still, San Miguel Mission, with its two-storied double bell towers, California Mission–style façade, and sweeping buttresses, remains one of the loveliest and largest of the older churches in New Mexico.

The Angel at the Gate

In 1800, when new settlers began rebuilding the town of Socorro, Apache raids were still very much a threat. Damaged as it was, the old church building with its thick walls and high windows still provided refuge to the townspeople. During one such raid, instead of attacking the town and church, the Apaches inexplicably turned and fled. A captured Apache warrior later explained that their raiding party had seen a tall man wearing great wings and wielding a huge silver sword standing guard over the door of the church. Who else could it have been but St. Michael the Archangel? The church has been dedicated to its guardian ever since.

The Buried Treasure

San Miguel Mission, Socorro.

In the early days, the original mission church at Socorro was graced with an altar rail and chalices made from solid silver mined in the nearby mountains and fashioned by the Indians. Before fleeing from the revolt in 1680, the priests dismantled

their beautiful altar rail and buried it, along with other valuables, somewhere in the vicinity. Despite a map drawn by one of the priests, the treasure has never been found.

✝ Santuario de San Lorenzo, Bernalillo

Las Fiestas de San Lorenzo have been celebrated in the town of Bernalillo every August for more than three hundred years. It was on St. Laurence's feast day (August 10) that the Pueblo Revolt occurred, and the Spanish settlers who had fled their haciendas for El Paso del Norte never ceased giving thanks for their safe deliverance that day.

In 1540, Francisco Vásquez de Coronado made his winter headquarters near the town now known as Bernalillo after his fruitless search for gold at Zuni Pueblo. At the time of Coronado's visit, there were twelve Indian villages in the immediate area. Coronado claimed them all for Spain and named them the Tiguex Province. By the time Don Juan de Oñate came through in 1598, most of the Tiguex pueblos had been abandoned. The area was only sparsely settled by the Spanish in the years before the Pueblo Revolt, but it was one of the first to be resettled after the 1692 reconquest. De Vargas himself named the town Bernalillo in 1695.

There seems to have been a small church at Bernalillo in its early days, though it was served by priests from Albuquerque (some fifteen miles to the south) and nearby Sandia Pueblo. In 1857, Bernalillo finally got its own pastor and a larger church was built. Originally called Nuestra Señora de los Dolores (Our Lady of Sorrows), the church was one of forty-five built under the watchful eye of Bishop Jean Baptiste Lamy. This church has the distinction of being one of the few Gothic-style churches in New Mexico that is built of adobe, a material that Bishop Lamy disliked. On this pretty church, the combination works. The church has double bell towers with elaborate gables painted in a striking light blue. The rose window and wooden door in the church's façade are also trimmed in blue.

In 1970, a modern church was built alongside the older one to serve the growing parish. In 1993, to commemorate the three hundredth anniversary of the Fiestas de San Lorenzo, the older Nuestra Señora de los Dolores Church was rededicated as the Santuario de San Lorenzo.

Los Matachines

Los Matachines is a traditional dance from Spain that tells the story of the triumph of Christianity over paganism. The dancers assume roles in the drama and wear elaborate costumes similar to those of mummers. In New Mexico, the dances have evolved over the years, incorporating Mexican and Indian themes. The dances remain religious in nature and are usually performed on liturgical feast days. Many of the New Mexico pueblos perform Los Matachines at Christmas and on the feasts of their patron saints. In Bernalillo, *los matachines* (the term refers to the dancers as well as the dance) parade through the streets of town, accompanying the procession of the bulto of San Lorenzo.

✝ La Capilla de San Antonio, Los Lentes

The land where the village of Los Lentes and its neighbor, Los Lunas, now stand was once part of Isleta Pueblo. The town of Los Lunas was primarily settled by prominent Spanish families, while the nearby farming community of Los Lentes has roots that include both Spanish settlers and Isleta Indians.

It has been speculated that La Capilla de San Antonio (The Little Chapel of St. Anthony) was named for the original patron of the church at Isleta Pueblo. When the mission was rebuilt after the Pueblo Revolt, its name was changed to San Agustín; many Isletans, however, never lost their preference for San Antonio. The church is called a *capilla* though it is actually quite sizeable. Records seem to indicate that there was already a church on a plaza called San Antonio in 1790. The church originally had a flat roof and a clerestory window, which is still visible in the church's

Facing:
Santuario
de San Lorenzo,
Bernalillo.

La Capilla de San Antonio, Los Lentes.

attic. The pitched roof was added in 1912. The bell towers were added in the 1860s as part of what some call Bishop Lamy's "Frenchification" project.

Today, the cruciform-shaped church—covered in whitewashed stucco during the 1970s—is, like many historic churches of the era, in need of repair. Still, it remains a beautiful building and an important part of the community. As a mission of San Clemente Parish in Los Lunas, Mass is still said at San Antonio every week. The people of Los Lentes remain dedicated to their church. For his feast day in June, new clothes have traditionally been created for the *bulto a vestir* (clothed statue) of San Antonio, which was probably brought to Los Lentes—along with other adornments for the church—when the railroad came through in the 1880s. Each year the statue is carried from house to house, where the rosary is said. The procession then proceeds to the church, where the fiestas continue.

✝ Nuestra Señora de la Luz, Cañoncito

The tiny hamlet of Cañoncito (Little Canyon), fifteen miles southeast of Santa Fe, first gained fame as the last station on the Santa Fe Trail. Perched at the edge of Apache Canyon, Cañoncito is just five miles from the Glorieta Pass, long known as the gateway to the eastern plains. During the Civil War, decisive battles were fought in the area.

The church, Nuestra Señora de la Luz (Our Lady of Light), was built in the 1880s. The small structure—today a mission of San Antonio de Padua Parish in Pecos—is made of adobe and covered in white lime plaster. A single wooden belfry sits atop its bright red pitched roof. An old cemetery surrounds the church and is lovingly maintained by the community.

The Santa Fe Trail

Like no other byway in America, the Santa Fe Trail inspires images of romance and adventure, of cowboys and covered wagons, Manifest Destiny and the call of the Wild West. In reality, the trip was probably more exciting in the telling than in the actual experience, since most of the nine hundred miles between Kansas City, Missouri, and Santa Fe were through the flat grassy plains of the midwestern prairies. Still, how excited those early travelers must have been to finally reach the weird and majestic landscape of eastern New Mexico, to move through the red rock walls of Glorieta Pass, knowing when they reached the last station stop at Cañoncito that they would soon be at the end of the trail.

While New Mexico was still a Spanish colony, it was isolated from the rest of the world, including the United States, since Spain forbade foreign trade of any

Nuestra Señora de la Luz, Cañoncito.

kind. With Mexican Independence in 1821, the trade restrictions were lifted and goods and settlers began pouring into the territory. In the past, supply caravans from Mexico had made the trip up the Camino Real only every three years. Suddenly, goods and people arrived on the Santa Fe Plaza every day. These were the boom years in Santa Fe, the years of gambling parlors, dance halls, and saloons. In the 1880s, the railroad came through New Mexico, and the heyday of the Santa Fe Trail gradually ended.

The Civil War in New Mexico

In 1861, Confederate soldiers from Texas made their way into New Mexico, hoping to seize Fort Union and make the territory their own. Both Santa Fe and Albuquerque briefly fell. In March 1862, however, New Mexico's Union-affiliated troops destroyed a Confederate supply train near Cañoncito and bested the rebel army at a bloody battle at Glorieta Pass that's been called the Gettysburg of the Southwest.

San José, Anton Chico

The small town of Anton Chico is best known for its role in the Lincoln County Wars. Although William Bonney—Billy the Kid himself—frequently visited Anton Chico, it is the church, San José (St. Joseph), that played a larger part by hosting the weddings of several of the players involved. In 1880, Sallie Chisum—daughter of cattleman John Chisum, leader of one of the factions in the conflict—was married at San José; some say she was an old sweetheart of Billy's. That same year, Pat Garrett, known as the sheriff who captured and killed Billy the Kid, celebrated his marriage there to Apolinaria Gutiérrez.

Originally settled on the banks of the Pecos River in the 1820s, by the latter half of the century Anton Chico was a busy town surrounded by thriving cattle and sheep ranches. The church was built in 1857 by Father Fayet, one of the priests brought to New Mexico from France by Bishop Jean Baptiste Lamy. Though built of adobe, the church has two square bell towers with tall, cross-topped steeples, reflecting the Gothic style preferred by the French priests of that era. Stained glass windows were added during a renovation after a fire in the 1920s.

Billy the Kid and the Lincoln County Wars

Cattlemen versus merchants, posses, gunslingers, outlaws—nothing says "wild west" like the Lincoln County Wars. In the years after the Civil War, Lincoln County covered the large area of southeastern plains that had developed into rich

San José,
Anton Chico.

ranchlands. In the 1870s, two factions vied for control of Lincoln County's economy. On the one side were merchants J. G. Murphy and J. J. Dolan, who not only ran Lincoln's only store but also had a lock on the cattle trade. On the other side were the cattle barons headed by John Chisum. On Chisum's team, known as the Regulators, was a man named Tunstall who planned to open another store in town. Tunstall's murder by a Lincoln County deputy, likely ordered by Dolan, set off three years of violence. One of Tunstall's employees was the famous outlaw known as Billy the Kid. Riding with the Regulators, he vowed to avenge Tunstall's death, which he did—by ambushing and killing the sheriff.

In 1881, Governor Lew Wallace reestablished peace in Lincoln County by offering amnesty to most of the participants. But for Billy the Kid—whose exploits were already famous—a $500 reward was offered. He was captured by the new Lincoln County sheriff, Pat Garrett, and was tried and sentenced to hang. Billy escaped on his way to his execution but was shot and killed by Garrett at Fort Sumner.

✝ San Francisco, Golden

In 1540, Coronado searched all over New Mexico and never found any gold. It seems he missed the Ortiz Mountains south of Santa Fe. In 1828, years before the California Gold Rush, deposits of placer gold were discovered in the streambeds of these hills. Before long, mining camps sprang up in the area. Eventually the camps became towns, which were later absorbed into the town called Golden in 1879. It may not have been one of the fabled Cities of Cibola, but in its day, Golden—situated on the Turquoise Trail between Santa Fe and Albuquerque—was a thriving town with a school, a post office, and several stores and saloons. It wasn't long, though, before the miners' gold pans were coming up with less and less gold. By 1928, Golden was a ghost town.

The church of San Francisco was built in the 1830s, soon after the first wave of mining camps settled in. It was restored in the 1960s by the noted New Mexican priest and historian Fray Angelico Chavez. Though the mining town is long gone, the lovely little church still stands in its gorgeous mountain setting.

San Francisco,
Golden.

PART THREE

The Capital City

"The Holy Faith of St. Francis"

✠ San Miguel Chapel, Santa Fe

As early as AD 1300, ancestors of Pueblo Indians lived on the south bank of the Santa Fe River. By the dawn of the following century, however, they had already moved elsewhere. The next people to make this area their home were Tlaxcalan Indians who journeyed from Mexico with Don Juan de Oñate's 1598 settlement expedition. It seems that when the party reached the high deserts of northern New Mexico, the Spaniards went north to San Juan Pueblo while these Indians settled in what is now known as Santa Fe's oldest neighborhood, the Barrio de Analco (Neighborhood beyond the River). When Governor Pedro de Peralta moved the Spanish capital from San Gabriel (near San Juan Pueblo) to the other side of the Santa Fe River in 1609, the Tlaxcalans were already building the chapel of San Miguel over the kiva of the abandoned pueblo, a sacred site the Indians recognized as a power spot. The new capital was named Santa Fe (Holy Faith). The full name of the city is La Villa Real de la Santa Fe de San Francisco de Asís (The Royal City of the Holy Faith of St. Francis of Assisi).

Facing:
San Miguel Chapel,
Santa Fe.

San Miguel was the first church built in Santa Fe, and—with its 1610 construction date—claims to be the oldest church still in use in the United States. In its early days, San Miguel was used not only by the Indians of the Barrio de Analco but by all of Santa Fe, Indian and Spanish alike. After the *parróquia* (parish church) was completed in the 1630s, San Miguel was reduced to a hermitage—that is, a chapel without a full-time pastor, used only for prayer and for services on special days.

There has been speculation that the chapel now standing on Old Santa Fe Trail is not the original structure built by the Tlaxcalan Indians in 1610. Certainly the church has been rebuilt several times and its façade has changed markedly over the centuries. The question is whether the walls themselves were ever completely razed. Did Governor Luis de Rosas (who apparently did burn the infirmary next to the chapel in 1640) make good on his threat to tear down the chapel? Was the church destroyed in the Pueblo Revolt? Were the old walls leveled before the church was rebuilt in 1710? The events prior to 1680 remain a mystery for the most part: all documents in Santa Fe pertaining to the Spanish were burned in a great bonfire on the Santa Fe Plaza during the revolt. There is reason to believe, however, that though the roof of San Miguel was torched (and likely everything made of wood inside the chapel destroyed), the walls were still standing after the 1692 reconquest.

One of the first things Governor Diego de Vargas did upon his reentry into Santa Fe was to inspect San Miguel. Santa Fe needed a chapel—and a home for the wooden statue of the Virgin Mary (afterwards known as La Conquistadora) he'd brought back with him from El Paso del Norte. Apparently the walls of San Miguel were still standing, since De Vargas ordered the Indians to rebuild the roof of the church immediately. Unfortunately, the icy December weather made a trip to the mountains for timber impossible. The project—at first postponed until spring—was delayed for another seventeen years.

In 1710, New Mexico's devout and wealthy governor, Don José Chacón Medina Salazar y Villaseñor (who also bore the title of Marqués de la Peñuela), personally donated two thousand adobe bricks to rebuild San Miguel. An inscription on the ceiling beam supporting the choir loft states that building was erected under the

Facing:
The sanctuary at San Miguel Chapel. This beautiful altar screen, constructed in 1798, was covered with white kitchen paint in the 1880s by a misguided Christian Brother who wanted to give the chapel a more European look.

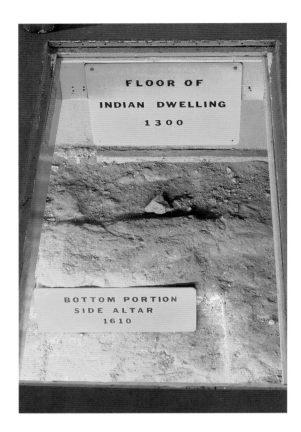

FLOOR OF
INDIAN DWELLING
1300

BOTTOM PORTION
SIDE ALTAR
1610

The 1955 excavation revealed the chapel's original floor as well as that of an ancient pueblo.

leadership of the Marqués in 1710. Nonetheless, many insist that the church was rebuilt using the existing 1610 walls.

Most of the Tlaxcalans had not returned to Santa Fe after the reconquest. San Miguel served as Santa Fe's military chapel until the construction of Our Lady of Light on the Santa Fe Plaza in 1728. For the rest of that century, San Miguel once again fell into disuse and disrepair.

In 1798, San Miguel received a face-lift. Mayor Don Antonio José Ortiz of Santa Fe paid for much-needed repairs to the old church, and commissioned the *reredos* (altar screen) that is in place at the chapel today. The Solomic Columns on either side of the screen—inspired by the Bernini columns at St. Peter's in Rome and once a popular feature of New Mexico reredos—were carved by local craftspeople. The panels contain a variety of eighteenth-century paintings, including the top center panel of St. Michael the Archangel, painted by Don Bernardo Miera y Pacheco in the 1750s. The panel of St. Teresa of Avila was probably painted in honor of Don Diego de Vargas, whose grandmother was a cousin of the popular Spanish saint.

In 1859, Archbishop Jean Baptiste Lamy bought the chapel and gave it to the De La Salle Christian Brothers, whom he had recruited to open a school for boys. The brothers made additional repairs and improvements, including a wood floor and altar rail. By 1887, however, the expense of maintaining the building—which had been badly damaged by weather, particularly by a freak earthquake in 1872 that destroyed the bell tower—became too much for the Christian Brothers. When they reluctantly announced that they planned to tear down San Miguel, funds and support poured in from the town's citizens, who wanted the church preserved. A new roof was put on the chapel, the bell tower was rebuilt, and stone buttresses were placed on the front and side of the building to support the buckling adobe walls.

A 1955 archeological study revealed the remains of the ancient kiva over which San Miguel was built, as well as more than two hundred graves beneath its floors. Most remains are believed to be those of Tlaxcalan Indians, although several priests and local dignitaries were also buried there. Legend has it that San Miguel is the final resting place of Don Diego de Vargas, although his ghost is not one of the many said to haunt San Miguel Chapel.

The Tardy Governor

In the early days of the settlement, battles raged between secular and religious authorities throughout the colony, and Santa Fe was no exception. One day in 1628, Governor Felipe Sotelo Ossario came late to Sunday Mass at San Miguel. On his way to his seat at the front of the church, the governor passed many of his officers, their heads bowed in prayer. After the service was over, Governor Sotelo reprimanded his officers for not standing at attention as he passed them. According to a document found in the archives at Mexico City, Sotelo said, "I swear to Christ, any day, even though it be at the elevation of the Host, you must rise and stand at attention [as a sign of respect to me] . . ." For this blasphemy (putting courtesies to himself above respect due to the Mass), Governor Sotelo was brought before the Inquisition at Santa Cruz. Unfortunately, it is not known what the Inquisition decided: all other documents pertaining to the case were destroyed in the Pueblo Revolt bonfires.

The Angry Governor

In another series of incidents some twelve years later, another governor also came into conflict with the Franciscans at San Miguel. This was Luis de Rosas, the angry governor who had burned down their infirmary and threatened to raze the church as well. Two friars from San Miguel, seeking to make peace, journeyed across the river to the Palace of the Governors on the Santa Fe Plaza. Instead of receiving them, Governor Rosas had them badly beaten. Striking a priest was a serious offense. Rosas was excommunicated from the Church, arrested by his own men, and ordered to stand trial before the Inquisition. The night before he was to be taken to Mexico City, an angry mob stormed his jail cell and killed him.

The Controversial Bell of San Miguel

According to Brother David, a Franciscan in charge of San Miguel Chapel in 1915, San Miguel's bell was cast in Spain in 1356 by Christians hoping for St. Joseph's aid in their battles with the Moors. Christian citizens, it is said, donated their gold and silver jewelry and household items to fashion the bell, which had the sweetest peal in all of Christendom. St. Joseph answered their prayers and the Moors were expelled from Spain. The bell later found its way to the New World to aid in the Spanish Crown's Christianization efforts there, and eventually was brought to Santa Fe by a member of De Vargas's reconquest party.

Others say that story is preposterous, that the bell was cast in 1856 in Chamisal (a tiny village on the High Road to Taos) by Francisco Lujan, a well-known bell maker, and that the date on the bell was actually changed from 1856 to 1356 by chipping at the metal. The age of the bell is currently being investigated. There is reason to believe that the earlier date (unlikely as it may seem) may be the real one. In any case, it is a beautiful bell, and can be seen and heard inside the Chapel of San Miguel.

✝ Santuario de Guadalupe, Santa Fe

Guadalupe is a village in Spain where a cowherd, guided by a vision of the Virgin Mary, found a statue of the Virgin that had been lost for six hundred years. But this older story has been eclipsed by that of an Indian peasant named Juan Diego who, in the earliest days of Spanish missionary work in New Spain, claimed to have seen the Virgin Mary on a hillside near present-day Mexico City. The image familiar today as Our Lady of Guadalupe appeared on Juan Diego's cloak as a sign to the bishop there. The cult of the Virgin of Guadalupe spread quickly, and soon she was hailed as the "Queen of Mexico." Many churches have been dedicated to her, especially in

Hispanic communities; the first and most famous one in the United States is the Santuario de Guadalupe in Santa Fe.

The santuario was probably built in the latter part of the eighteenth century, although some accounts place its construction date much earlier. Originally built in a simple adobe style with a cruciform plan, the massive church, located on the south bank of the Santa Fe River (across town from San Miguel), has undergone many renovations over the years. Its famous altar screen, with its large center painting of Our Lady of Guadalupe, was commissioned for the church in 1783; like other sacred artworks of the period, it was rolled up and carried on muleback over the Camino Real from Mexico City.

The church was used only sporadically until 1880, when the Denver and Rio Grande Railroad came to town. With the depot just a block away and the tracks running right past the church, it's appropriate that Archbishop Lamy designated the Guadalupe Santuario as the new parish church to accommodate all the English-speaking immigrants pouring into Santa Fe on the railroad. It was at this time that Lamy—never a fan of Spanish Colonial architecture—had the church completely remodeled to look more European. A pitched roof was added, a tall spire replaced the original bell tower, and windows were cut into the thick earthen walls.

In 1922, a fire destroyed the spire, most of the roof, and parts of the interior. Happily, the beautiful altar screen escaped damage. The resulting repairs gave the Santuario de Guadalupe yet another update, this time in the California Mission style.

Our Lady of Guadalupe, seen here on the center panel of the santuario's *altar screen, is the most popular image of the Virgin Mary in the Southwest.*

Santuario de Guadalupe, Santa Fe.

A new parish church was built next door in 1961, and again the santuario fell into disuse. Rather than tear it down, the Archdiocese leased the old church to the Guadalupe Historic Foundation in the 1970s. This group again renovated the exterior, this time with the idea of restoring the building to its original style as much as possible. The santuario was returned to the care of the Archdiocese of Santa Fe in 2006. Mass is celebrated there on the twelfth day of every month in honor of the Feast of Our Lady of Guadalupe.

The reredos *at the Santuario de Guadalupe tells the story of Juan Diego's 1531 visions.*

Juan Diego and the Virgin

On December 9, 1531, a poor Indian peasant named Juan Diego saw an apparition of the Virgin Mary on a hill outside what is now Mexico City. Juan Diego, a very devout man, was a fifty-seven-year-old fairly recent convert to Christianity: he'd been baptized only seven years before by one of the first Franciscan missionaries in the New World. He often walked the many miles to the nearest church; he was on his way to Mass when he first saw the woman who identified herself as the mother of Jesus. She had dark skin like his, spoke to him in his own dialect, and called him "my son" and "Juanito." She told Juan Diego to go and tell the bishop that she wanted a chapel built on that spot, the hillside called Tepeyac. Juan Diego obeyed, but the bishop did not believe him. If this was true, he said, let the Virgin Mary send a sign as proof.

A panel from the reredos at the Santuario de Guadalupe. Here, the peasant Juan Diego first sees the vision that will become known as Our Lady of Guadalupe.

Juan Diego was afraid to tell the beautiful lady who had spoken to him so kindly about the bishop's request. It wasn't until three days later that he ventured near Tepeyac, and when he did, the Virgin was waiting for him. She was not angry. She told Juan Diego to pick the roses from the hillside and deliver them to the bishop. Juan Diego was confused: it was December and the ground was frozen. But, sure enough, there on the snow-covered desolate hillside were red roses in full bloom. He gathered them into his cloak and hurried back to the bishop. When Juan Diego opened his cloak, the roses spilled at the astonished bishop's feet. But this was not the only sign: on the inside of Juan Diego's humble cloak was the image of the woman Juan Diego had seen, the image we know today as Our Lady of Guadalupe.

✝ Cathedral Basilica of St. Francis of Assisi, Santa Fe

When Bishop Jean Baptiste Lamy arrived in New Mexico in 1851, his first cathedral was the old adobe parróquia on the east side of the Santa Fe Plaza. This was at least the third adobe church to stand on this site. The first, a tiny mud edifice named for Our Lady of the Assumption, was built soon after Don Pedro de Peralta moved the capital from San Gabriel to Santa Fe in 1609. This tiny church, described as a hut by the Franciscan Alonzo de Benavides, was torn down and rebuilt by him in the 1620s. While the new parróquia was being built, the people of Santa Fe attended Mass at San Miguel Chapel, just across the Santa Fe River. The new church, finished in the early 1630s, was destroyed less than fifty years later during the Pueblo Revolt. The third parróquia—this time dedicated to St. Francis of Assisi—was not built until 1714. By the time of Bishop Lamy's arrival, this church was well over one hundred years old.

New Mexico had long been part of the Diocese of Durango, Mexico, but when the territory became part of the United States in 1848, a new Vicariate Apostolic (which was elevated to a diocese in 1853 and an archdiocese in 1874) was created for the American Southwest. Lamy, a Frenchman who had spent ten years working in the Diocese of Cincinnati, was named the first bishop of Santa Fe—the capital and then-largest city in the territory (which at that time included Arizona and Colorado as well as what is now New Mexico). Bishop Lamy had ambitious plans for his new home and lost no time implementing them. He brought new priests over from France to revitalize the parishes—not without conflict with the old guard of New Mexican priests; he planned schools and recruited the Sisters of Loretto and the Christian Brothers to teach them; and, notably, he began a program of building and rebuilding New Mexico's churches. The forty-five churches built under Lamy's tenure reflected the Frenchman's personal preferences in architecture. Suddenly, buildings of brick with gothic arched windows began appearing in New Mexico, and many existing churches were given European makeovers with the additions of Romanesque towers and stained glass windows. The bishop was known for his distaste for churches "built of mud," and made it his mission to bring to the territory what he deemed to be more appropriate places of worship.

From his first days in Santa Fe, Bishop Lamy dreamed of a grand stone cathedral like the one in his childhood home of Clermont-Ferrand in France. The Southwest needed a cathedral, he felt; by his standards, there was no important church west of St. Louis or north of Durango, Mexico.

The Romanesque cathedral that now stands in Santa Fe is the fulfillment of Bishop Lamy's dream. It didn't happen overnight. Such an ambitious project required money, and it wasn't until 1869 that the cornerstone for the new church was laid. Architects were brought in from France to build the stone edifice Lamy designed, which was inspired by the church of his childhood. The new structure was built around the old parróquia, using it as a support. When the nave was finally finished in 1884, the older church was torn down, brick by brick, from the inside.

Lamy did not live to see the completion of his dream, though he blessed the cathedral in 1886, a year after he retired. He died in 1888 at his retreat just north of Santa Fe, and is buried under the main altar at St. Francis Cathedral. The cathedral

Right:
Cathedral Basilica
of St. Francis
of Assisi, Santa Fe.

Facing:
The nave and
sanctuary at the
Cathedral Basilica
of St. Francis
of Assisi.

Above:
Archbishop Lamy's
private chapel at
his retreat north of
Santa Fe is now
part of the resort
known as The
Bishop's Lodge.

Facing:
Our Lady
of Peace in her
place of honor in
La Conquistadora
Chapel in the
Basilica Cathedral of
St. Francis of Assisi.
The reredos *was*
made from a portion
of the altar from the
1717 parróquia.

was formally consecrated in 1895 by Placid Louis Chappelle, the third Archbishop of Santa Fe. The tall wooden spires originally planned for the church were never built.

In recognition of the important role that both the cathedral and the Archdiocese of Santa Fe have played in the history of the Catholic faith, St. Francis was named a basilica in 2005 and is now formally known as the Cathedral Basilica of St. Francis of Assisi. The building of the cathedral and the life of Archbishop Lamy were immortalized in Willa Cather's fictionalized classic *Death Comes for the Archbishop*.

La Conquistadora

A chapel on the north side of St. Francis Cathedral is all that remains of the 1717 adobe parróquia. This lovely old space is home to the oldest representation of the Virgin Mary in the New World: the statue known as La Conquistadora.

The small wooden statue is thought to have been brought to Mexico from Spain in the early 1600s. It was carried to Santa Fe by Fray Alonzo de Benavides,

La Conquistadora spends one week every June at her former home, the Rosario Chapel.

who came north to oversee the New Mexico mission efforts in 1625. Her first home in New Mexico was the parróquia on the Santa Fe Plaza that bore her original name: Our Lady of the Assumption.

During the 1680 Pueblo Revolt, La Conquistadora was rescued by the *sacristana* (caretaker) of the parróquia, Josefa López Sambrano de Grijalva, and was carried by the fleeing Spanish to El Paso del Norte. Don Diego de Vargas himself brought the statue back to Santa Fe when he and his army reconquered New Mexico in 1692. A chapel was built for her in 1693 on the spot where Don Diego and his men were said to have spent their first winter in Santa Fe. Rosario Chapel was named after another of the statue's appellations: Our Lady of the Rosary. Every year in June, La Conquistadora returns to Rosario Chapel (which was rebuilt in 1810) for fiestas and special services before being returned in a great procession to her present home in La Conquistadora Chapel in St. Francis Cathedral.

The statue, made of willow, is twenty-eight inches tall and is a *bulto a vestir*—a "clothed" statue—with an extensive and beautiful wardrobe, as is fitting for the "Queen of the Kingdom of New Mexico and the Villa of Santa Fe."

La Conquistadora is the most common of her many names, and refers to the conquistadors who brought her to New Mexico as well as to her role in the peaceful reconquest of the territory in 1692, which the Spanish soldiers attributed to her intercession. Today, she is known as Our Lady of Peace.

✝ Loretto Chapel, Santa Fe

One of the most popular tourist stops in Santa Fe is the lovely chapel built for the Sisters of Loretto on Old Santa Fe Trail just south of the plaza. Built during the construction of St. Francis Cathedral, the Loretto Chapel is home to the famous "miraculous staircase."

Loretto Chapel, Santa Fe.

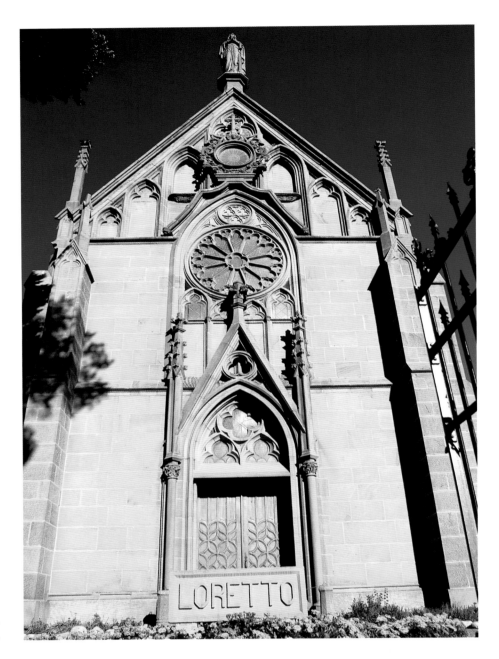

Loretto Chapel,
Santa Fe.

When Bishop Lamy came to Santa Fe in 1851, one of his first missions was to recruit teachers. He wrote scores of letters to religious teaching orders, pleading for assistance. The first to accept his challenge were the Sisters of Loretto. These nuns, a teaching order based in Kentucky, agreed to send seven of their sisters to

The sanctuary at
Loretto Chapel.

Santa Fe. Bishop Lamy himself traveled to Kentucky to accompany the sisters on the treacherous journey across the Santa Fe Trail. Only five nuns completed the trip— their Mother Superior died and another sister fell sick and had to return to Kentucky after the group was exposed to cholera. The others continued bravely westward; the sisters arrived in Santa Fe in 1853 and opened the Loretto Academy for Girls. In 1853 and again in 1855, more nuns made the journey and joined their sisters in New Mexico.

In the late 1860s, Bishop Lamy hired Antoine Mouly, a French architect, to build St. Francis Cathedral. The bishop suggested that the sisters take the opportunity to have him design a chapel for them as well. The nuns raised the necessary funds and also took Lamy's suggestion to model their chapel after his favorite small church in Paris, Sainte Chappelle, which had also been designed by Mouly. The façade of the narrow Gothic-style chapel is built of stone. Inside, plaster walls were painted to resemble stone and tile, and other trompe l'oeil features were used with great effect. The elegant altar with its tall pointed archway is actually made of wood that has been painted to look like marble. Likewise, the statues and elegant Italian Stations of the Cross are not made of carved marble but are created from molded marble dust that has been fired and hand-painted.

The Miraculous Staircase

The most interesting feature of the chapel is its beautiful and mysterious spiral stairway. The chapel was designed with a lovely wood-railed choir loft lit by a magnificent rose window, but with no staircase to reach it. In those days, both in Europe and in the old mission churches in New Mexico, this wasn't unusual. Many choir lofts were reached by ladder, which took up much less room than a flight of stairs. In the case of the Loretto Chapel, which was used almost exclusively by nuns wearing long flowing habits and girls in long dresses, a ladder was hardly practical. Unfortunately, the architect, M. Mouly, had returned to France because of bad eyesight and his son, whom he had left behind to finish his work, died a few years later—some say of typhoid or some other fever, others say of poisoning. A third French architect, François Mallet, seems to have been shot and killed by Bishop Lamy's nephew, who suspected the architect of having an affair with his wife.

All of which sordid goings-on left the good Sisters of Loretto with a problem—with two problems, actually: not only did they need to have a staircase built, it also had to be a specially designed staircase. The design of the small chapel

Facing:
The miraculous staircase at Loretto Chapel. The rose window can be seen behind the choir loft.

didn't leave room for a conventional stairway, so it was necessary to construct one that would fit in the small space available.

From the very beginning, the Loretto nuns had dedicated their chapel to the care of St. Joseph, the husband of Mary. Who better to ask for help than the humble carpenter saint? The nuns said a novena—a nine-day prayer for special intentions—to St. Joseph. At the end of the nine days, the story goes, an old man with a donkey appeared at the chapel and agreed to build the sisters their staircase. In some versions, the stairs are built overnight. In others, they are built in the week before Christmas. More often, it is reported that the job took several months. What is beyond dispute is that when the staircase was completed, the man vanished from the area without being paid for his work.

The result of his labor is a work of art and genius that has only recently been replicated. The spiral stairway is built without a center support of any kind, attached only to the floor of the chapel and to the choir loft itself. It has thirty-three risers and is constructed without nails, using only small, perfect wooden pegs. To add to the mystery, no local merchant reported selling any lumber for the project. More than that, to this day the type of wood used has never been definitively determined.

Who was the mysterious carpenter? Although several local families have claimed that the old man was a grandfather or uncle, he has never been identified. The Sisters of Loretto and others speculate that the man—gray haired and bearded, leading a donkey—might have been St. Joseph himself.

Whoever he was, the carpenter built the stairway without a banister. The narrow and steep spiral stairway was terrifying to climb for the poor sisters and their students. St. Joseph or not, after seven years the sisters commissioned another carpenter to build them a graceful railing that in no way detracts from the beauty of the original staircase.

After educating Santa Fe's young girls for more than one hundred years, the Loretto Academy closed in 1968. Today the chapel is privately owned and lovingly maintained. It is a popular venue for weddings and concerts and is visited by hundreds of tourists every year.

Cristo Rey, Santa Fe

Cristo Rey (Christ the King), the beautiful church at the top of Canyon Road in Santa Fe, incorporates many of the features that make New Mexico's churches so special: thick adobe walls supported by buttresses, a clerestory window, and an exterior balcony. This church, however, is not a well-preserved relic of Spanish colonial days but a relatively new church built in 1940 by renowned New Mexico architect John Gaw Meem.

The construction of Cristo Rey achieved three purposes: first, to serve the growing population of parishioners on Santa Fe's east side; second, to provide a permanent home for the magnificent stone reredos that had previously graced Our Lady of Light, the military chapel on the Santa Fe Plaza that had been torn down in 1860;

Cristo Rey Church, Santa Fe.

finally, as the archbishop announced on Easter Sunday of 1939, to commemorate the four hundredth anniversary of the discovery of the "New Kingdom of St. Francis."

Cristo Rey is the largest adobe structure in the United States, with a nave 125 feet long and 40 feet wide. The walls, as thick as nine feet in places, were made from some 200,000 adobe bricks, each made by hand by the parishioners themselves. Local craftsmen also carved the corbels (the ornate corner braces supporting the vigas), which were harvested from New Mexico forests. The result is a beautiful example of Pueblo Revival architecture, a style that incorporates the elements of the Spanish Colonial style as well as Pueblo Indian building forms.

The Stone Reredos

The ceiling of the sanctuary of Cristo Rey church is thirty-three feet high—just tall enough to accommodate the magnificent stone altar screen the church was designed to showcase. The beautiful reredos was commissioned in 1760 by Governor Francisco Antonio Marin del Valle for the military chapel known as La Castrense, which was being built on the south side of the Santa Fe Plaza. The artist is not documented but is thought to be Bernardo Miera y Pacheco; the carvings probably were done by Mexican artisans employed by the governor. The figures in the panels include St. Joseph, St. James the Great, San Juan Nepomuceno, St. Ignatius Loyola, and St. Francis Solaro, as well as the Virgin Mary and God the Father.

The altar screen, made of white stone harvested in the hills above Santa Fe, was probably carved inside La Castrense (also known as the chapel of Our Lady of Light), which served Santa Fe's military community for almost one hundred years. After 1848, a military chapel was no longer necessary: the American soldiers stationed at Fort Marcy were mostly Protestant, and Catholicism was no longer the official religion of the territory. Bishop Lamy sold the now-dilapidated chapel in 1859 to raise money for his cathedral. The altar screen and other church relics were taken to the parróquia and afterwards stored in St. Francis Cathedral.

Cristo Rey provides the perfect setting for this priceless work. Moving the heavy stone reredos—even in the three pieces in which it was made—was no easy

Facing:
The stone reredos,
now at Cristo Rey
in Santa Fe, was
carved in 1760.

task. Legend has it that the designer intended more space between the top of the altar screen and the ceiling of the sanctuary, but that the height of reredos was miscalculated. The story is apocryphal, but it is true that the huge reredos just barely fits into its space behind the altar. Another story, told by Meem's secretary and biographer, relates that after the three large sections of the reredos were finally secured behind the altar, Meem went home for lunch. Tired after a long morning spent adjusting the panels, he sat down at the table, only to jump to his feet in mid-bite. Meem told his astonished wife that something was wrong at the church. Rushing back to Cristo Rey, the architect found workmen diligently scrubbing the stone altar screen with stiff brushes, oblivious of the old and fragile paint on its panels. Thus did John Gaw Meem save the delicate pastel colors of the old reredos.

John Gaw Meem

The man many call the father of Santa Fe Style was not born in New Mexico but rather arrived in the 1920s in order to recover from tuberculosis at a local sanatorium. John Gaw Meem fell in love with the landscape and architecture of New Mexico, and called Santa Fe home for the rest of his life. It was Meem who created the Pueblo Revival style that revitalized the centuries-old building traditions unique to New Mexico. In addition, Meem was a founding member of the Society for the Preservation and Restoration of New Mexico Mission Churches, and personally oversaw the restoration of the churches at Acoma Pueblo and Las Trampas, among others.

Resources

Selected Bibliography

Bunting, Bainbridge. *Early Architecture in New Mexico.*
Albuquerque: University of New Mexico Press, 1976.

Cash, Marie Romero. *Built of Earth and Song: Churches of Northern New Mexico.*
Santa Fe: Red Crane Books, 1993.

Cather, Willa. *Death Comes for the Archbishop.*
New York: Alfred A. Knopf, Inc., 1927.

Chauvenet, Beatrice. *John Gaw Meem: Pioneer in Historic Preservation.*
Santa Fe: Museum of New Mexico Press, 1985.

Chavez, Fray Angelico. *My Penitente Land.*
Santa Fe: William Gannon, Publisher, 1979.

Chavez, Fray Angelico. *The Santa Fe Cathedral of St. Francis of Assisi.*
Santa Fe: Schifani Brothers Printing Co., Inc., 1947; updated, 1995.

Chávez, Thomas E. *An Illustrated History of New Mexico.*
Niwot, Colorado: University Press of Colorado, 1992.

DeBorhegyi, Stephen F. and E. Boyd. *El Santuario de Chimayó.*
Santa Fe: Ancient City Press, 1956.

Drain, Thomas A., N. Scott Momaday, and David Wakely.
A Sense of Mission: Historic Churches of the Southwest.
San Francisco: Chronicle Books, 1994.

Gavin, Robin Farwell. *Traditional Arts of Spanish New Mexico.*
    Santa Fe: Museum of New Mexico Press, 1994.

Hooker, Van Dorn. *Centuries of Hands:*
    An Architectural History of St. Francis of Assisi Church.
    Santa Fe: Sunstone Press, 1996.

Jenkins, Myra Ellen, and Albert H. Schroeder. *A Brief History of New Mexico.*
    Albuquerque: University of New Mexico Press, 1974.

Kay, Elizabeth. *Chimayó Valley Traditions.*
    Santa Fe: Ancient City Press, 1987.

Lehmberg, Stanford. *Churches for the Southwest:*
    The Ecclesiastical Architecture of John Gaw Meem.
    New York: W. W. Norton & Company, 2005.

Lucero, Thomas L., and Thomas J. Steele.
    Religious Architecture in Hispano New Mexico.
    Albuquerque: LPD Press, 2005.

Montoya, Joe L. *Isleta Pueblo and the Church of St. Augustine.*
    Isleta Pueblo: St. Augustine Church, 1978.

Murphy, Dan. *Salinas Pueblo Missions.*
    Tucson: Southwest Parks and Monuments Association, 1993.

Noble, David Grant, ed. *Salinas: Archaelogy, History, and Prehistory.*
    Santa Fe: Ancient City Press, 1993.

Padilla, Carmella, ed. *Conexiones: Connections in Spanish Colonial Art.*
    Santa Fe: Museum of Spanish Colonial Art, 2002.

Poling-Kempes, Lesley. *Valley of the Shining Stone: The Story of Abiquiu.*
    Tucson: University of Arizona Press, 1997.

Prince, L. Bradford. *Spanish Mission Churches of New Mexico.*
    Cedar Rapids, Iowa: Torch Press, 1915.

Sheehan, Archbishop Michael J., ed. *The Cathedral Church of St. Francis of Assisi.*
    Strasbourg, France: Éditions du Signe, 2003.

Sheehan, Archbishop Michael J., ed. *Four Hundred Years of Faith: Seeds of Struggle—*
    Harvest of Faith: A History of the Catholic Church in New Mexico.
    Albuquerque: Starline Printing, 1998.

Steele, Thomas J. *Santos and Saints: The Religious Folk Art of Hispanic New Mexico.*
    Santa Fe: Ancient City Press, 1974.

Index